S0-ADV-053

WHEN
GOD
TALKS BACK

Madness or Mysticism?

TASHA MANSFIELD, PH.D.

Published by
Centauro Publishing

7230 N.W. 58th Street
Miami, Florida 33166
Tel: (305) 436-1159
Fax: (305) 436-0974
E-mail: centauro.miami@ibm.net

Copyright ©1998 by Tasha E. Mansfield

All rights reserved. No part of this book may be reproduced
in any form or by any electronic or mechanical means, including
photocopying, recording, and information storage and retrieval
systems, without prior permission in writing from the author.

First printing September 1998

Editor: Gustavo Nieto Roa

Cover art by Michael Leas

Graphic Design: M. Zamora - L. Santofimio

Printed in Colombia by
Tercer Mundo Editores S.A.

ISBN: 1-893083-00
Library of Congress Catalog Card Number: 98-87958

This book is dedicated
to my daughter,
Mia Michele,
a rare flower
in the magical garden
of the Divine.

Acknowledgments

While writing a book is a solitary pursuit, it cannot come to fruition without the contributions of many people.

First and foremost, I wish to thank my father, Dr. Murray Mantell, for his perennial wisdom, my mother, Rose Mantell, for her ceaseless generosity of spirit, and my sister, Dr. Andrea Seidel, for her reassuring strength and support. I am also indebted to the rest of my family, whose optimism, steadfast faith, and love made this book possible.

To Dr. Shyam Kashyap, an angel on earth, words alone could never express the depth of my love, admiration, and deep appreciation.

A special thanks to my editor, Cynthia L. Jenney. Her tireless efforts and deep commitment to excellence are without equal. I also wish to thank Michael Leas for his visionary cover art. My most heartfelt gratitude to David Freed, a gentle soul and cherished friend, and to my publisher, Gustavo Nieto Roa, a kindred spirit who believed in me and made my dream a reality.

To all of the gifted and luminary friends who have supported me by endorsing this book, James Redfield, Dr. Bernie Siegel, Dr. Edgar Mitchell, Dr. Carlos Warter, Dr. Gerald Jampolsky, Dr. Diane Cirincione, and Jane Chaplin, you are forever in my heart.

Contents

Introduction

> *"What is mind? No matter. What is matter?*
> *Never mind. What is soul? It is immaterial."*
> —*Hood*

The perplexing question posed in the title of this book is one that has been pondered in the minds and hearts of people throughout the world since antiquity. Before we can begin to broach the task of finding an answer to this question, we first need to know that there is more to life than what we can perceive with our five senses. We need to know with unflinching certainty that there is definitive and profound meaning and purpose in our routine daily existence. This vital requisite is an incessant yearning, conscious or unconscious, in all humanity. We will never be thoroughly satisfied with the belief that life, all life, is arbitrary and random.

Mysticism, simply defined, is the nature and development of spiritual consciousness. This book is about exploring an approach to life that asserts the primacy of the inner world of spirit and the ability to use that pathway to make contact with "All That There Is." It is a book that aims to answer the pressing questions that must be asked about our life's mission and our individual place in the world.

Are the mystic illuminations that have been exalted throughout the ages authentic glimpses into true being and ultimate reality? Is there a magical, non-physical world that parallels the one that we can readily perceive and with which we are intricately interconnected? Or are people who make claims of conscious visitations and intimate familiarity with other realms mad? This book examines these enigmatic questions in an attempt to differentiate madness from mysticism. Ultimately, the direction we must face to find the answers to these profound questions is not east or west, but inward.

Within these pages is the story of a personal journey into the elusive world of the Divine. This book is a mystical travelogue, a guidebook that escorts the spiritual sightseer on a detailed, first-hand tour of breathtaking, magical vistas that are not on any map. The trek to this wondrous realm cannot be made by way of the usual modes of transportation. The only available transport that can reach this mysterious plane of existence is our mind. Just as the radio is used as a tool to receive and consolidate radio waves, our mind can be trained to tune to the frequency of this other reality.

Once there, you will discover an exotic, unspoken language, one that is composed of symbols, signs, and universal significance. In this realm, fluency can be achieved with mere understanding.

My excursion was certainly not an exclusive experience. Many others have found themselves to be suddenly in sync with the life-movement of the universe and ensconced in an intimate rendezvous with Grace. But as our technological society continues to contribute to a slow and methodical weaning from the belief in a divine intelligence, we have slipped away from knowing this reality directly.

We mistakenly think that we have not yet developed the implements and apparatus needed to perceive unseen realms. With the invention of the microscope, we suddenly glimpsed into a miraculous microscopic world that was previously unknown. Our "reality" changed as a result of this discovery. But the instrument that we must use to perceive this other dimension has been with us all the time—the imponderable machinery of our own mind. It is as if we have been looking at water contained in a glass without acknowledging that a vast ocean is its actual source.

The catalysts for my immersion and preoccupation with this pursuit were a combination of a deepening dissatisfaction with my traditional training as a medical psychotherapist, the limited results I was achieving with my patients utilizing this restricted training, and most significantly, a profound, spontaneous spiritual experience. This experience has had a staggering impact on my life. From that moment on, the world has never looked quite the same. The shock wave from this first "divine earthquake" registered a whopping 9.5 on the psychological Richter scale. The aftershocks, which continued for years, gradually led me away from my previous analytical and shortsighted attitudes and viewpoints.

As a consequence of this profound spiritual experience, I felt compelled to embark upon years of soul searching and study to obtain at least some fragment of understanding of the unseen forces that influence our daily lives. The quest to penetrate the mysteries of these genuine healing energies became my steadfast goal. The material for this book gradually developed after spending those years pondering, researching, and introspecting.

For almost a century, psychology has played a huge part in contributing to the fragmentation of the human being by suggesting directly or indirectly that the spiritual side of our nature is either nonexistent or, when in full expression, symptomatic of mental illness. Of course, the textbooks imply that religion, per se, is perfectly acceptable. The difficulty arises, however, not when a person believes in and speaks to God, but in those moments WHEN GOD TALKS BACK.

As a mental health professional, I am now treading on the proverbial eggshells. It is no wonder that the estimated tens of thousands of people who have actually had some sort of genuine mystical or religious experience have chosen to remain silent and ashamed, lest they be labeled by the well-intentioned psychological community as disturbed or insane and subsequently treated with suppressive medication. Mainstream science and psychology—and even some organized religions—typically regard contemporary mystical and religious phenomena as pathological symptoms, delusions, or myths. They judge people who experience these events as being in need of "curing" to achieve normalcy. These negative and erroneous labels have trickled down into the public psyche with disastrous consequences. It is entirely possible that through the eventual application of science committed to the exploration of realms now unquantifiable and with our own open hearts and minds the dividing line between mysticism and madness shall become entirely clear.

We need to know our spirituality not just from an intellectual perspective; we need to learn how to BE our spirituality. This will not materialize until the biased viewpoints held by the mental health profession are reevaluated and reworked to acknowledge and support the existence of spiritual realms and the divine nature of our being.

Mystics have always believed that the true reality of life may be found in the deep interior of our essential nature and that it is possible for all of us to experience that feeling of unity that connects the inner and outer realms. Living life this way enables us to perceive ordinary, mundane objects and events in an extraordinary way and enter into previously unimagined domains of consciousness.

In biblical times, experiences of non-ordinary states of consciousness were not only accepted but revered as a blessing from the Divine. Illuminated thinkers throughout history—Plato, Albert Einstein, William Blake, Walt Whitman, and Carl Jung, to mention a few—have reported spontaneous mystical experiences, which they describe as union with God or the merging of the soul with the Absolute. Most have reported having visions or hearing a divine or celestial voice. After much self-analysis in the face of scrutiny by their peers, they ultimately reached the conclusion that human beings have a vast potential to experience reality in ways that pragmatic and analytical thinking have shunned. These philosophers also firmly believed that the biblical stories told for two thousand years are, for the most part, literal in their descriptions of God speaking to Moses, Christ, and other saints.

Taboos and stigma against visions and voices first arose when the scientific method became predominant in the nineteenth century and scientific proof could not be found for these profound metaphysical events. According to most scientists, experiences of enlightenment and illumination are merely the result of a vivid imagination, superstition, or delusion. This myopic perspective regarding arcane and unexplainable universal mysteries has contributed to a stunting of society's spiritual growth.

Was it only in biblical times that people were able to converse and unite with God, have prophetic visions, and heal the sick? I think not. Our essential nature has not changed in two thousand years. We have always been and always will be spiritual beings enjoying a human existence.

Upon placing an ad in a national journal dedicated to science and spirituality, I received an avalanche of mail in response to a request for experiences perceived as spiritual, religious, or paranormal. Most respondents had never disclosed their divine encounters to anyone. They were thrilled to finally have someone willing to listen to their story and take them seriously. The overwhelming majority were sincere, stable people who told of extraordinary, poignant accounts of union with the Infinite and a subsequent personal metamorphosis.

There is a silent voice that speaks to us all. If we are willing to be still and listen, it will inspire and bring hope and profound meaning to those who are endeavoring to find peace of mind in this difficult and stressful world. Now is the time to bring our divine natures out of the dark shadows into the light.

It is my hope that these chronicles will help you discover that quiet voice within. As you leaf through these pages, you can decide for yourself the answer to the question in the title of this book. Which it is? Madness or mysticism?

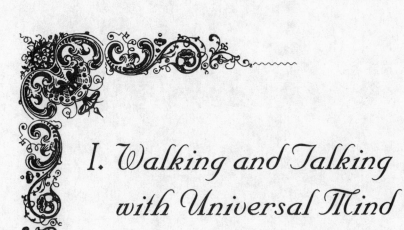

I. Walking and Talking with Universal Mind

Saga to Sanity: First Union

> *"Great wits are sure to madness near allied, and thin*
> *partitions do their bounds divide."*
>
> —*Dryden*

his book relates a very personal story. It is a mystical adventure story about an excursion into a previously unknown world, a miraculous world filled with the unveiled truths and principles that lie at the root of the creative process, a domain saturated with knowledge cloaked in symbolism, where the past, present, and future merge into one time and space. This is an elusive realm which, when entered, incites and kindles the process of transformation and faith. It is a dominion in which a profound relationship exists between all things, animate and inanimate, and divine grace is bestowed on any and all visitors.

My journey on the age-old path in search of self and the meaning of life is both idiosyncratic and universal. This is not only my unique story of retracing my steps back to my Source; it also exemplifies and parallels the experiences of all the others throughout history who have witnessed the remarkable vistas gracing the corridor between humanity and the Divine. This is the not-so-ordinary tale of an ordinary person who has treaded some of these ancient and well-traveled roads.

During my twenty-eight-year career as a practicing medical psychotherapist, I have been witness to a virtual sea of despairing souls, all asking essentially the same aching questions: "Why am I suffering?" and "How can I find happiness?" The frantic search for contentment and peace of mind has escalated over the past few decades as our society increasingly moves toward economic pursuits and away from spiritual fulfillment and the true meaning of life. For most, the relentless quest for happiness has become a fruitless reconnaissance mission sought through alcohol and drugs, endless mental distractions, or illusions of security, whether financial or emotional.

I must admit that I, too, for a time was caught in the mirage of the American Dream, that myth of personal identity and success defined as the sum total of one's possessions and accomplishments and the speed at which they can be acquired. At the age of thirty-eight, I arrogantly believed I was at the pinnacle of my career and the zenith of my personal growth. I took great pleasure in my achievements and identified with them as a reflection of who I was and how I wanted to be perceived. Of course, this identity would shift like sand in the desert as my roles in life rapidly changed from friend to mother to doctor to professor. In hindsight, I was not on solid ground despite my erroneous conviction to the contrary.

It was precisely at this time in my life when the psychic earthquake began beneath me. This mystical tremor suddenly convulsed and collapsed all the meticulously built structures of belief systems and identities that I had constructed brick by brick around me like a fortress. I was soon to discover how these crystallized ideas had held me captive and emotionally imprisoned for decades.

"Self is the only prison
that can ever bind the soul."
—Henry Van Dyke

Although I had married, raised children, and traveled extensively, the overwhelming majority of my time and energy had been devoted to academic goals and career pursuits. During the very formative college years, like most,

I established and shaped my belief systems about life. My outlook tended to border on the sardonic and cynical, as I perceived the human condition as being so seemingly arbitrary and pointless. In my view, people were born, ran madly about trying to accomplish things, suffered at some point, reproduced … and then it was over. As much as I struggled to try to make some sense of it all, there seemed to be no rhyme nor reason for our existence, or at least, none that I could see. Unfortunately, as the years passed, my early, shallow convictions developed further into unimaginative attitudes that were based on the limited premise "What you do is who you are." Of course, with this type of thinking, it became of utmost importance to me to have a successful career and project the image of someone who possessed wealth, influence, and prestige. Career success became my primary goal and motivator.

My postgraduate psychology training was essentially traditional with a strong Freudian bias. In the 1970s, most universities, and psychology departments in particular, suppressed originality and thwarted innovative, creative thinking. My training was standardized and steeped in outdated tradition. New ideas that challenged the status quo were quickly squelched as if the entire institution of education were hanging by a fragile thread that would snap with any pressure. The degree of conformity required to be successful and make it through the program was difficult for me to accept, but I was eager to become a doctor, so reluctantly I submitted to the established norms.

In spite of my rebellious attitude, or perhaps because of it, education and exploration had always been a passion. There was so much that I wanted to know. Though I had hoped to find the knowledge I was seeking in the institutions of higher learning, I ultimately graduated no wiser nor more scholarly, but awash in disillusionment and disappointment. The gnawing questions that I had had about human nature had not been answered. It seemed that after years of study all that I had accomplished was the memorization and regurgitation of innumerable theories and speculations. On the day of my graduation, submerged beneath an ornamental smile and ensconced in the subterranean depths of my being were the sad murmurings of questions unanswered.

Born into a Jewish family in the late 1940s, I was exposed to frequent anti-Semitism as a child. Racial hatred, or hatred of any kind, never made any sense to me, but I was affected by it, nevertheless. Spiritual or religious doctrine was not discussed in my family, so by young adulthood, I had jettisoned conventional Judaism with the exception of the practice of selected and mechanically executed rituals.

The exposure that I had had through the years to other religious faiths failed to spark my interest in the least. I was generally unconvinced by much of the dogma in organized religions. If I had any opinions about spirituality at all, these ideas tended to be agnostic, if not atheistic. Frankly, I looked upon people who were deeply religious as rather weak and in need of a psychological crutch. I had come to the conclusion that devoutness reflected irrationality, superstition, and even emotional instability and that religion served only to create separation and conflict rather than harmony. After all, so many wars had been fought over religious beliefs. Pompously, I thought of myself as rising above the superstitious axioms. Ultimately, I remained faithful to logic, practicality, and science alone.

The most crucial developmental years and by far the most influential were the turbulent late 1960s and early 1970s. This was a period of enormous social and spiritual upheaval during which the existing order and government came under attack from questioning minds and fledgling countercultural revolutionaries. Eastern customs and practices invaded the West, bringing ancient spiritual traditions, which the music of the times helped to integrate deeply into the public psyche.

The Hippie generation, of which I fancied myself a member, led the student revolts and anti-Vietnam War protests which formed the roots of the sweeping social change that eventually blossomed into the Equal Rights Amendment, civil rights, and the end of the war. The space program was literally blasting off, and the country was reaching for the moon and the stars. During this revolutionary era, I became the quintessential bra-burning, protesting, anti-establishment feminist so typical of the times. Woven into my hair was the signature wreath of flowers; my body, draped in naval-bearing tie-dye; my feet, frequently bare.

But even as I was entrenched in the peace movement, I was not the least bit peaceful inside. My heart was heavily burdened with the civil unrest and chaos of the war. Violence, murder, and brutality were beyond my comprehension. I was a young, socially conscious idealist largely unaware that my need to be politically active was an attempt to bring meaning into my life. Despite the cynicism and petulance that occasionally lacerated my hope for the future of the country, strong altruistic motives that were fostered during these times propelled me to choose a career that directly involved helping people. Psychology was the choice that ultimately prevailed.

With the passing of this season in history, my youthful idealism, too, seemed to fall away. The sixties and seventies had unraveled, leading to the weakening of institutions such as marriage and the family, a strengthening of government, massive economic growth, and enhanced individualism. I soon found that my personal political interests were relegated to a remote and distant concern.

Utopian, ivory-towered aspirations and a somewhat hedonistic lifestyle were pushed aside by the harsh reality of economic survival. My rose-colored glasses were replaced with prescription eyewear. Employment, education, and child-rearing duties succeeded the heroic deeds of my youth. Valiant acts now consisted of finding pre-schools, passing exams, and paying the rent.

By my mid-twenties, I had already married, divorced, and become resigned to single parenthood. The father of my child, due to his habitual insobriety, abandoned us and eventually died in an alcohol-related accident. My attempts to juggle a full-time education, full-time employment, and full-time parenting frequently led to periods of complete and utter exhaustion. The pressures of daily life were grueling and relentless. I just kept putting one foot in front of the other in the obsessive pursuit of my goals, which were largely professionally and materially motivated. Had I stopped to think about all the responsibility, I would have collapsed!

All the while, something of paramount importance was lacking inside of me. Something was missing. I could not put my finger on it. Contentment was just a theoretical notion. I felt jaded and steeled by the hardships. To cope, I turned the knobs on the control panel to automatic pilot and barreled through life unconsciously not knowing any other way to be.

Eventually, through tenacious perseverance, I accomplished my goal of becoming a doctor. As I was well on my way to realizing the American Dream, I believed that life would now be easier and my struggles would be over. Naively, I thought that at last I would be in full control and the master of my destiny.

Nothing in my wildest dreams, nothing in my personal or scientific background could have prepared me for the disorienting but exhilarating expedition that was about to unfold, the effect of which was extraordinary, instantaneous, and permanent.

❧❧ *Initiation*

It was the end of an ordinary weekday that had been filled with the usual array of mundane activities, responsibilities, and work, work, work. I had been spending long hours in the office as my patient caseload and teaching duties had rapidly expanded. There never seemed to be enough time to complete all of my obligations. As usual, I was stretched thin.

The standard maze of paperwork surrounded me, but I was determined to make some headway in eliminating part of it. I resentfully committed myself to several more hours in the office to take care of administrative tasks. In the midst of this absorption in my ongoing dysfunctional relationship with dozens of unkempt files, I was suddenly jolted by a faint, though distinct voice:

"Please leave the office now."

Quite startled, I rapidly scanned the room looking for the person to whom the voice belonged. No one was there. Relieved but uneasy, I took several deep, tenuous breaths mingled with uneasy laughter. I promptly discounted whatever I thought I had heard and resumed the task at hand.

Barely a moment had elapsed when again I heard, more distinctly this time, the same verbal instruction:

"Please leave the office now."

In an instant, my composure gave way to increasing apprehension and confusion as to the actual location or source of this voice. That very moment, I realized that this undeniable sound had originated inside of me. With that thought, a formidable shroud of anxiety enveloped me in a mild pandemonium. Thankfully, my training as a psychotherapist helped me to manage my emotions, so despite the agitation, I launched into an analysis of the situation and mentally reviewed numerous possibilities and explanations for what was occurring. The choices ranged from the practical to the absurd, but the most likely explanation was that I was overstressed and simply becoming unhinged.

At the time, I had little understanding or knowledge of mystical concepts. My existing belief systems about paranormal events were saturated with psychological pigeonholes. My ability to comprehend what was happening was limited to a narrow framework of diagnostic options. Of course, a more open-minded and visionary outlook was nonexistent.

With much trepidation, I continued to appraise and evaluate myself. I quickly packed up my belongings and headed for the imagined safety of the parking lot. The sunny day that marked the Spring Equinox was coming to an end. As the darkness of evening was beginning to creep in, I left the building and climbed into my car.

Ten minutes elapsed as I drove, and all seemed normal. I tried not to think about this strange thing that had just happened and successfully eliminated all thoughts of it from my mind. Breathing a sigh of relief as I neared my home, I turned due west onto a road aptly named Sunset Drive.

As I turned the corner, I was dazed by the most magnificent and radiant sunset I had ever seen. Just on the rim of the horizon sat a huge, blazing, fiery golden ball, shimmering as if it were a heat mirage, vibrating in waves and sending a profusion of colors cascading into the sky. Encircling the circumference was a luminous corona that graced it like a radiating halo. The air suddenly felt particularly and uncharacteristically invigorating and electric.

During this twinkling moment on its arched path across the sky, the sun was positioned over the centerline of this road exactly due west. My entire field of vision became tinged with lavender and pink. I looked very carefully. This shining globe seemed to have an uncommon brilliance and golden luminosity. At that instant, the sparkling, gilded shimmer flashed forward from the sun down the road directly toward me, casting a metallic light all along the street in front of me. I was barely breathing!

Shafts of copper-colored, laser-like beams radiated out, piercing the clouds. I felt infused by the penetrating rays of the sun's energy, which inexplicably mingled with my own electrified vitality. It seemed as if the sun were putting on a spectacular show just for my benefit as I continued to be bathed in gleaming columns of warm, roseate-colored light. I could not help but be seized by the revelation that this bright sphere was the source of all life. I understood immediately why the sun was once so worshipped.

My mind raced with a mass of jumbled thoughts. What was happening? I had witnessed ten thousand sunsets during my lifetime, but never one like this. I felt disoriented yet buoyant.

An ancient Jewish saying begins by suggesting that a person should wear clothes that have two pockets. In the first should be a piece of paper which reads, "I am but dust and ashes." In the second pocket, the ancient wisdom advises, there should be a piece of paper on which is written, "For me the world was created." At that moment, I fully understood the true meaning of those words. I felt a deep, newfound inner wealth.

Again, the voice spoke:

"Keep the light, even in the darkness."

Tears began to flow—both from the powerful emotions welling up inside me and a rising fear of the unknown. In retrospect, I would say that I was equally divided between the awe and the fear. I trembled with a hodgepodge of confusion. What could this mean? What was happening to me? Who "on earth" was speaking to me?

I pulled off to the side of the road and sat in my car for what seemed to be an eternity, watching the setting sun and laboriously pondering my circumstances. Everything in my field of vision looked uncommonly clear, pristine, and glistening. The sunshine reflected a dazzling glare from the leaves of the trees. So emblazoned were they with this golden luster that the trees seemed to be on fire. Could this be what Moses experienced when he was on Mount Sinai and encountered the bush that was "burning" but not consumed? Did he see a bush so aglow with cosmic force that he chronicled the incident as fire? My thoughts rambled on as I groped for answers. I sat almost paralyzed with confusion.

A progressive and unremitting kaleidoscopic array of colors beamed from the sun, spreading glazed, lustrous hues across the sky as if it were a living painting. Streaks of clouds formed surrealistic brushstrokes tinted with a vivid, phosphorescent luster. Just then, a sheath of tranquillity slipped over me like a fine silk cloak, and I soon felt my equilibrium return. I had never witnessed such beauty. I had seen a sunset for the very first time!

Back in the refuge of my home, I continued to feel more at ease and in control. Rapt in thought as I brewed a cup of tea, all I wanted was my well-known version of normalcy. But then, once again, the voice returned, speaking to me periodically, often with long intervals in between. Endowed with a didactic quality both in the tone and content, it addressed areas of personal and spiritual growth and provided guidance about my future development. Despite the fact that absolutely nothing threatening was said, I harbored a growing fear that sent shivers through every fiber of my being.

By mid-evening, the expansive feelings had escalated, and my mind was flooded with euphoric revelations. Random knowledge steadily streamed in as I was bombarded with a sense of seeing things AS THEY ARE. I can only describe this intellectual illumination as being akin to accessing the vastness of the Internet with my mind. It seemed as if the universal databases were at my disposal. The feeling was analogous to plugging myself into an electrical outlet. I was the plug; the outlet, Universal Mind, the term I use for the unfathomable intelligence we call God.

The seed thought for this book came from inspiration on this first night, though the concept of a book on spirituality and mysticism was foreign and inconceivable at the time. Failing to comprehend the extent of what was being communicated and why and how this interchange was taking place, I felt increasingly more queasy and worried.

As I sat quietly in a chair, mostly trying to calm myself, it seemed, metaphorically, as if I were sitting in a vast library. Through some mystical process of osmosis, a magical and subtle absorption of the knowledge and wisdom contained in these "books" continued to seep into my mind for the remainder of the evening. My thoughts were ablaze with information and realization. It was overwhelming! Finally, quite exhausted, I fell asleep.

That night I dreamed as never before. Vivid, powerful dreams emanated from deep within, seemingly with the explicit purpose of giving expression to my heart's true desires. A sense of holiness and sacredness pervaded my dream state along with an unusual and quizzical vitality. Astoundingly, I remained fully conscious and completely lucid throughout. I knew exactly where I was and understood that everything that was happening in this dream state was just as real as in my waking hours.

Strangely, as I dreamed, I sensed the existence of another dimension, some other inconceivable place, yet one as familiar as what I would normally refer to as "reality." For the first time, I experienced the borderline between our waking consciousness on the physical plane and consciousness—tapping into Universal Mind—as we sleep. I found myself in that peripheral region where the mystical and the psychical meet. The usual canyon between the two now seemed only a thin divide. The phenomena, ideas, the life, and knowledge of this other dimension registered on my mind and imprinted on my brain as memories.

I dreamed that I had ascended to the heavens and was ceremoniously floating through space, gently caressed by a benevolent universe with the stars as my glittering jewels and the moon as my nightlight. With merely a thought, I was able to will myself from place to place and adjust the height of my travels. At times, I would find myself in a small, adobe cottage sitting on a floor mat and in rapt conversation with an aged oriental sage. Other times, I would be in the midst of a large group of people, all clothed in white and peacefully interacting.

Several of the dreams that I had that first night later proved to be prophetic, though not of much consequence. But what struck me the most and scrambled any remaining sense of stability was that upon waking, I knew without a doubt that wherever I had been and whatever I had experienced were REAL, not my normal reality, but some other enchanting, gossamer realm that was also home.

A quirky trend developed at this time. I began to remember my dreams every single morning. Very frequently, the dream would exactly correspond to the headline in the morning newspaper. I did not know what to make of this whimsical anomaly, but after a time, I found it entertaining.

Upon awakening the next morning, everything appeared normal and familiar. Soon after breakfast, however, I began to have what I can only describe as visions. Otherworldly images flashed at lightning speed through my awareness. It might be argued that these visions were only products of an active and vivid imagination, but clearly, they were not. The experience can only be described as a type of supersensual intuition, the result of the contact between my finite being and the Infinite Being in which we are all immersed.

The images were "flashforwards" rather than flashbacks. This communication from some divine part of me insisted that I pay attention to its imploring messages from obscure inner depths. These images were methodically placed before my consciousness like an exhibit of foreign postcards. The mail carrier was unmistakably Universal Mind. Some of this special delivery mail I wanted to "Return to Sender." Glimpses of unwelcome future events, including the time and circumstances of my own death, fleetingly darted through my mind like momentary vignettes of a movie premiere.

"Have you ever asked for that instruction
by which we hear what cannot be heard,
by which we perceive what cannot be perceived,
by which we know what cannot be known?"
—*Henry David Thoreau*

Opportunities for growth and learning come to everyone, but all too often we falter and fail to take full advantage of them. Often, probably daily, opportunities specifically designed by unfathomable forces arrive to assist us in our spiritual growth. Why is it that we tend to take the path of least resistance, the path of our lower-level desires, the one that, although most familiar, will produce the least threatening change in our life and also the least development? We always have an option when faced with this dilemma. The choice is either to follow the tugging of our soul, which would lead us to our highest good, or the seduction of the emotions, guiding us to satisfy desires.

At this turning point in my life, I was facing this internal showdown. I kept resisting the call of the soul because of my ignorance and fright of the unknown and unfamiliar. Limited thinking groomed by years of training in the scientific method obscured my understanding of what had been so benevolently communicated to me. Almost a year passed before I was finally able to delve into the profound teachings imparted to me.

The next day, I went to work as usual, but it was a far cry from a typical workday. Throughout, I was involved in an interior struggle, a futile attempt to maintain the status quo versus the coaxing and urging of my own spirit to enter into a life unknown. Little did I know that this was the beginning of an awakening which would lead to a new and more active plane of being, a changed and more personal relationship with my Source, and ultimately, a greatly enhanced ability to truly assist in guiding others toward self-healing and wholeness.

"Every creature is on its way to the highest perfection.
In each, there is movement from mortality toward Being."
—Meister Eckhart

That day in the office was astounding. The patients I saw, whom I thought I had known and summed up so well, were somehow different. But they had not changed; it was my perception of them that had radically shifted. I listened carefully to their words but heard through the words. I somehow knew to bypass their vocalized thoughts until I contacted the place inside of them that knew everything and had all the answers. The answers were just forgotten. I tried to help them remember.

As I looked at their faces as I had done so many times before, I saw a diffused white light dispersed around their heads and shoulders. I kept blinking my eyes to refocus but that just made the glow seem even brighter. "Could this be what the New Age folks call auras?" I wondered. Even while mulling over the question, I simultaneously knew that somehow that was exactly what they were.

Much later, while reading several nineteenth-century metaphysics books, I learned that emanations of light around the head and shoulders are, of course, not new. Museums are brimming with masterpieces depicting saintly people with these glowing, luminous clouds around their head. I came to understand that this light is the result of an effusion of energy emitted by the etheric body, or soul. We are electromagnetic beings who continuously radiate fields of energy laden with information about who we are. This is why certain people affect us either positively or negatively.

Before my eyes, one by one, these patients were transformed. They were no longer patients; they were living vitality, radiant souls living in a dense physical body which was, in part, the source of their troubles. I now viewed the problems that weighed so heavily upon them and at times incapacitated their lives with an untarnished understanding. I gained an invaluable and treasured piece of wisdom that day that has since brought much peace of mind. The fundamental and evident truth is that adversity is in fact prosperity in disguise, as it always has a divine purpose. Sorrow can be our best educator. With the newfound insight, I now saw rainbows in their tears.

> *"Tears are often the telescope through which*
> *men see far into heaven."*
> —*Beecher*

The limitations of traditional psychotherapy were now graphically and glaringly clear. How could I possibly help anyone truly heal if spirit, the vital substance of which the universe is made and the essential part of humankind, was utterly ignored? No wonder depression has reached epidemic proportions and so many people are plagued by profound inner voids. We fail to see who we really are, and the blindness is debilitating.

The visions did not continue for the remainder of the day but rather metamorphosed into a formless intuition that guided and directed me in matters pertaining to the present and future. Oddly enough, the usual perception of linear time had been altered. The past, present, and future were juxtaposed and simultaneously occurring, seemingly all in one place. This would be analogous to sitting in Carnegie Hall and hearing the dim traces of all the symphonies that have ever filled the chamber as well as the music presently playing and all the sweet-sounding harmonies that ever will be played. I was in a state of awe!

Everything that was happening was so utterly alien to me. I vacillated back and forth about its reality and still held the option that I was ill at bay. However, my scientifically trained mind was incredibly intrigued with it all, so I began to dictate my experiences as they occurred on a miniature tape recorder that I carried with me. There came a turning point, however, when my skepticism begun to wane. I had seen something with physical eyes and a mind that was opening that vanquished much of the doubt and uncertainty.

In the sanctuary of home later that day, I decided to venture outside for a walk. A magnificent, breezy Florida day greeted me. The weather was perfect—clear, flame blue skies and crisp, cool air. Strolling in my neighborhood, I happened to look up for a moment, and I suddenly became deliriously ecstatic by what I saw. The atmosphere surrounding me was no longer merely invisible, empty space. The air was permeated with minute, luminescent specks whirling in circular patterns in an enthusiastic dance with one another. Rapidly gyrating, they saturated and infused everything and incited the surrounding plants to a pulsating aliveness. I was invigorated and almost intoxicated by the joy of it. These particles were so brilliant that it was puzzling to me that I had never seen them before.

Somehow, I knew that every speck possessed its own intelligence and that, combined, they shared a collective and complementary consciousness.

Each one was like a miniature sun orbiting in its own sphere while simultaneously being part of the whole. It was a glittering mosaic of energy and intelligence and an obvious metaphor for the light of humanity. I continued to stare at this collaborative symphony of light and movement and soon realized that space itself was a living entity. The space between the specks was also vitalized and possessed a benevolent and incomprehensible substance.

I found myself briefly worrying about the effects of air pollution on this astonishing spectacle of light and movement. I wondered about the impact it might have on our health and well-being. Not wanting to dwell on these concerns, I quickly turned my attention back to watching "dancing air."

The splendor of that living light became my compass, guiding me in this adventure and reconciliation with reality. As I began to open more to the grace of the moment, along with this outward light sprang a fountain of inward light that struck my soul with such force that again tears flowed. But this time they were tears of joy and jubilation because, for that split second, I had fused with the unity of all things. Physical boundaries no longer existed, and I could have no more harmed a blade of grass at that moment than myself. Everything that I could see, including my physical body, was imbued and nourished by these bright sparks of light. I knew that nature was always in perfect harmony. It is we that become out of sync with it.

Years later, after much study and pondering, I realized that these dazzling golden-white specks are what is known as "prana" in India or "chi" in China. Not yet widely recognized in the West, this is a vital force that emanates from the sun and is one of the main life-giving elements. I was fascinated when I noticed much later during another walk that hundreds of gnats were flying in the exact same pattern as the specks. I knew that this energy was so powerful that it influenced and compelled the gnats to arrange themselves in an identical pattern. Because of their brilliance and perpetual motion, these specks can be seen in infinite numbers darting about in the atmosphere, especially on a sunny day. The effect vaguely resembles that of the sun reflecting on water.

Several hours later, when this state of mind subsided (it seemed to come in rhythmical periods), the trained analytical aspect of myself had diminished and my spirit was so strengthened that I actually said to myself, "If this is madness, how incredibly wondrous it is!" The psychological literature says that madness is associated with a sense of falsity in one's existence. That day I had never felt more alive nor as real.

> *"See, the human mind is kind of like ... a piñata.*
> *When it breaks open, there's a lot of surprises inside.*
> *Once you get the piñata perspective, you see that losing*
> *your mind can be a peak experience."*
> —*Jane Wagner*

The Wordless Language of Universal Mind

> *"All of God's works are signs and expressions of His attributes; and thus it seems that all of physical nature is an expression and image of the spiritual world. All creatures are able to perceive truth and the nature of things only in images."*
>
> —*Johann Georg Hamann*

The next morning, very pensive and self-absorbed, I was leisurely gardening in my backyard. As my hands tilled the soil, I knitted together various theories about the spellbinding events of the previous day in an attempt to reach some semblance of order and understanding. Hypothetical and contradictory ideas gently lingered like reflections of that incredible sunset, slipping in and out of my thoughts.

As I meticulously clipped and pruned the rose bushes, I came to feel that I was on the cusp of adjusting to this novel awareness and synthesizing my ordinary life with these budding perceptions. Not only were all of my five senses greatly heightened, but I was also discovering new senses that I had not previously known. Touch, smell, hearing, and sight were all elevated and enriched in some unexplained way.

Just as I was getting comfortable with this newly found mindfulness, a curious and incessant barrage of mental and visual images was transposed onto my existing environment. What I mean by this is that the ordinary and commonplace things around me took on a divine and more profound significance. As I had experienced with my patients days before, I seemed to be able to see beyond the physical form and into the substance and essence of the object. Another layer of reality lay behind everything, just as the peeling away of the translucent skin of an onion exposes layer upon layer wrapped around an indistinguishable center.

A mere thistle possessed divine qualities; an insect, a touch of the sublime. And each had a very clear place and purpose in the cosmos. The environment began to communicate in a symbolic language, guiding and teaching me through the most mundane objects. The familiar and known seemed to pull me like a magnet into the ambiguous unknown. Strangely, I understood the interplay and rapport between the plants as they exchanged and expressed a mutual fellowship with each other. It was not anything at all like speech, but an interchange and reciprocity that was a form of thought. All of the vegetation was fully conscious, a much lower form of consciousness than human or animal, but sentient nevertheless.

I was experiencing a deep intuition that straddled two dimensions. An aspect of my mind seemed to be drawn toward perceiving almost everything in my environment as metaphorical and symbolic. This compelling force implored me to learn profound concepts and truths. The most inconsequential things were unmasked and became representations for meaningful lessons about life and the laws of nature. A trickling stream would emphasize the continuous fluidity of life and the importance of being free-flowing and changeable. Everything that caught my eye stimulated a blitz of information and lessons as the mysteries of life were gradually unveiled.

This dichotomy and the onslaught of superimposed impressions were so bizarre that I again began to become a bit concerned for my sanity. However, to my surprise, this odd binary perception did not make me feel fragmented. On the contrary, it had generated a sense of wholeness, within and without.

Periodically, I would reexperience a complete loss of separateness from all of nature. Despite this fusion, the boundaries of "myself" were clearly maintained. There just seemed to be less of me and more of "us" as I identified and remained in rapport with my surroundings. God was everywhere—in the rich soil, in the leaves of the trees, and in the filmy flight of the birds that soared overhead. I perceived that nothing was itself without everything else. Every cell in my being overflowed with compassion for all living things. My simple little garden in the midst of the city was metamorphosing into a Garden of Eden.

As I finished with the rose bushes, my attention was diverted to an old and well-worn wooden adirondack chair that sat on my back patio. I had owned this chair for years, and for some time it had remained in a sorry state of disrepair. As I became engrossed in this chair, I noticed that it looked the same as always on the surface, but another image overlapped onto it, an image of its prior life. In my mind's eye, I saw a majestic tree, a living monument that stretched to the heavens, alive with the nectar of the earth. It was an invincible giant, proudly basking in the sun. Converging with that image, I heard the moan of its agony as it was felled and mutilated. Here on my patio were the mummified remains, all that was left of this venerable natural spire. I felt grateful for its sacrifice. From that day on, I have never been able to look at furniture or trees in quite the same way.

As I continued to perceive and understand that everything was composed of the same cosmic substance, I became increasingly sensitive to my environment. I now saw everything as conscious and alive. Atoms and molecules accumulated cohesively to form solid objects, but what was holding those objects together was a limitless, inexhaustible intelligence and energy. This is not a novel idea, but one that has been evident to many theoretical physicists. But it is one thing to read about quantum physics and quite another to be able to "see" at the atomic level. I could not fathom how this was possible.

I became aware of an increased capacity to read a specific meaning into each symbol or object that attracted my attention. On an intuitive level, the same symbol that I was seeing would have a unique and possibly very different implication and communication to someone else because, apparently, each personality influences the interpretation of the messages emanating from Universal Mind.

The environment was teaching me, guiding me every moment. Everything—all objects and events—was a veiled divine ideal, a subtle impression registering on my mind. Through some unintentional shift in consciousness, I could now perceive an alternative reality which had always been eternally present, but which I was just now discovering because an interior light had miraculously been switched on.

Later that same day, when I went into town to do some errands, I came across a man cutting down a massive, aged oak tree with a chain saw. Still in a state of communion with Universal Mind, I actually FELT the severing of that body as if it were my own. I was in such an expanded state of mind and highly sensitive condition that it affected me dramatically, as if I had witnessed a murder. The unnecessary and senseless mutilation of a magnificent life form enervated me, and waves of sorrow erupted in an emotional epiphany. I immediately began to lament the destruction of the environment. It now seemed brutally criminal to harm another living thing. How impossible it would be for people to destroy nature, much less other human beings, if only they could see how alive and conscious it all is, how much a part of us it is, how much a part of it we are.

Why was all of this happening to me? The experiences were daunting yet irresistible. The consequences of these new perceptions were cataclysmic. I felt exhausted and emotionally pushed to the limit, but I had no choice but to press on.

I had been the recipient of a ubiquitous key that allowed me to cross the threshold of a cosmic door that lead into a world illumined with knowledge, wisdom, and light. This is akin to coming into contact with a psychic energizer that arouses the mind to recognize the true reality and purpose of life and the profound meaning hidden just below the surface of the physical world.

*"To the eye of the seer, every leaf of the tree is a page
of the holy book that contains divine revelation and he is
inspired every moment of his life by constantly reading and
understanding the holy script of nature."*
—Hazrat Inayat Khan

As a child, I used to read a magazine featuring a game with pictures of camouflaged animals and objects. The goal of the game was to sift through the illustration and find them. I would compete against myself with each new issue to see how quickly I could discover the concealed items in the drawing. The experiences I share here are essentially just like that. I had the same thrill of discovery and awe that I had had as a child.

There were moments, on this day, when my life had become that game. As I glanced around me, I seemed to be looking at my customary environment but, as I did, certain landmarks and directional markers would stand out and beseech me to contemplate them. It was if a magical filter covering my eyes screened out the mundane and enhanced the extraordinary.

The phenomenon of computer-generated three-dimensional illusions illustrates my newfound revelations and requires the same shift in perception. The computer is programmed to create a colorful design of lines and forms. With much concentration and a slight adjustment in awareness, what you at first see as a colored pattern soon exposes its dual nature as a picture within a picture.

As the day went on, objects in my environment—billboards or road signs for example—would reveal cryptic messages or mysterious underlying meanings. These double messages from things in the physical world were at first confusing, but they soon began to convey ideas that were of a profound and lofty nature.

It seemed that Universal Mind had clicked the remote control and changed the channel in my brain. A previously unknown clarity and agility of mind allowed for a new direction and openness in my thinking. I was receiving clear satellite reception from some unknown zone. A deluge of complicated and previously inconceivable abstract concepts surged through my psyche. The inundation of astonishing data was almost oppressive as the primordial mass of information begged for my attention. Eventually, I was able to surrender sufficiently and allow my mind to explore this unseen realm.

The noted Swiss psychologist Carl Jung devoted much of his work to the study of symbols. His contributions very positively colored the field of psychology with a metaphysical (meaning "beyond the physical") orientation regarding human nature. He believed that a word or image was symbolic when it implied something beyond its obvious and immediate meaning and that it could have a wider, more unconscious connotation that was unique and personal. Jung proposed the theory of syncronicity, the belief that meaningful and mysterious coincidences occur and that they are a manifestation of a universal order or universal law. In other words, nothing is coincidental. All events are orchestrated and coordinated by an inconceivable intelligence. The reasons behind this divine plan are unfathomable.

Since we have always used symbolic terms to represent concepts that we cannot define or fully comprehend, could this symbolic language actually be an aspect of the language of God? Is this possibly one way in which Universal Mind directly and personally communicates with us? It has never made sense to me that if such a vast, creative, and totally benevolent intelligence existed it would be so remiss as to fail to create a way to dialogue with humanity. Is it rational to think that we can speak to and communicate with a God that hears us but will not or cannot respond or communicate directly?

The Bible itself is written in symbolic language and in metaphor. For instance, Jacob's dream of a ladder, the top of which reached to heaven, is completely allegorical. The ladder symbolizes the ascent of humanity, while each rung represents an evolutionary phase upward toward full conscious realization. And Joseph's coat of many colors, which is described in the book of Genesis, may be a symbolic representation of the etheric garment we all wear, the various hues of each distinct, fantastically radiant aura. Perhaps the authors of the Bible understood the language of Universal Mind and wrote the scriptures exactly as they received them—symbolically. Even every number in the Bible has a mystical connotation. For example, the number seven represents the completion of a phase of development.

Perhaps, I thought, it is simply not possible for us to withstand direct contact with such an omnipotent energy while we inhabit our physical bodies. The effect just might be harmful to our bodies and our minds. Perhaps this Intelligence dilutes things a bit so that we can more easily assimilate them. It must be normal and natural to converse and interface with our Source, and it is only a matter of time before we will understand this concept more completely.

It was not easy for me to embrace these ideas. I wrestled for many years with various speculations and eventually became convinced of their validity through an understanding of the nature of dreams. When we dream, our unconscious mind communicates with us and selects symbols for the purpose of teaching and guidance. These symbols have meanings that are specific and pertinent only to the dreamer. By interpreting these abstract forms, we may discover profound parts of ourselves and the other divine dimensions that we visit during sleep. It is in this same way that we may receive symbolic guidance in our waking state.

"A mystical symbol is an expressible representation
of something which lies beyond the sphere of
expression and communication, something which
comes from a sphere whose face is, as it were,
turned inward and away from us. A hidden and
inexpressible reality finds its expression in the symbol.
The symbol signifies nothing and communicates
nothing, but makes something transparent
which is beyond all expression.
Where deeper insight into the structure of the allegory
uncovers fresh layers of meaning, the symbol
is intuitively understood all at once—or not at all."
—Gershom G. Scholem

This newly found ability to communicate with the Divine is not a special privilege reserved for me alone. Everyone experiences divine communication and syncronicity in some form or another.

Case in point is that of John F. Kennedy, Jr. Just after his marriage, he told a story at a luncheon in Oregon. He was staring out a window, wondering whether he should make a major life decision when his eyes were drawn to a billboard that said, "Just do it!" According to Kennedy, it was Nike's famous slogan that convinced him to take the plunge and marry. You might suggest that his experience was simply a fluke, but if you penetrate into the unique and personal meaning of a symbol, it can provide a means for the dormant and unconscious intuition to rise to the surface. Everyone has experienced this, and it is genuine divine guidance.

It is easy to just dismiss the belief in communication with the Divine as madness or superstition. My psychological training again initially hindered my understanding of the experience. Before all this happened, my only frame of reference for synchronous and metaphysical events was in the term "ideas of reference," used by psychiatrists to describe a psychotic state. It is defined in the *Diagnostic and Statistical Manual of Mental Disorders* as "the feeling that casual incidents and external events have a particular and unusual meaning that is specific to the person." I find it interesting that the feeling and thoughts considered to be pathological by this internationally utilized psychological manual could also be interpreted as a mystical experience.

The Egyptians used a written language of images and representations that is closer to the language of the universe than ours is. For reasons that completely baffled me, I was reading hieroglyphic-like symbols without any prior knowledge or experience. Unfortunately, my academic training had so dulled my ability to be open-minded and receptive that it almost prevented me from allowing the spontaneity and potentiality of tremendous learning from this imagery.

The capacity to read meaning into a symbol in the environment largely depends upon the amount of depth that is desired in daily life and the willingness to delve into the complexity of perceiving two realities at once. How willing are you to put aside fixed ideas about the world and open to receiving these symbols, the clothed thoughts that the spiritual borrows from the material plane? They are visible, external signs of an inner spiritual reality.

In ancient times, people routinely looked to omens for guidance and help with decisionmaking. Omens were thought to come in the form of birds, animals, or events, which were then received and welcomed as a personal message from the Divine. These emmisaries are not merely the result of primitive superstition; they are very specific, organized transmissions imparted from spiritual realms with the intention of assisting us. We are guided by a mysterious, omnipotent intelligence every second of every day. It is only our human arrogance that hinders us from knowing our Source directly.

The belief that people and nature freely and mutually communicate and dialogue is ingrained in Native American culture. Native Americans have experiences that allow the reception of messages from their natural environment because they are not only inclined to avail themselves of the communion and divine intercourse but also consider the harmonious exchange a gift of grace.

A recent example of divine communication through symbolic events was presented in the hit movie "Sleepless in Seattle." The plot of the film revolved around the main character's receiving signs that eventually guided him to his soul mate. I believe the success of the film was largely due to this enchanting premise. People want and need to believe that there is magic in life. And magic really does exist!

The mental shift that humanity desperately needs to make as we enter the twenty-first century involves the renewed perspective that the universe is not random and meaningless. In fact, everything that exists and occurs is meaningful and purposeful and geared to aid us in spiritual development. I emphasize the importance of symbols because their recognition and interpretation can result in increased contact with the soul and thus heighten one's sense of inner direction. Reading symbols can provide a means whereby dormant intuition can be stimulated into activity. When you exercise full awareness, you may sense the unique message and guidance that lie behind the color and form of which the symbol is composed.

As another illustration, I offer an anecdote from the days of my doctoral internship. For several years, I studied under the tutelage of Dr. Bernie Siegel, author of *Love, Medicine, and Miracles*. At that time, Bernie was a practicing surgeon at Yale New Haven Hospital. Fortunately, I had the opportunity to train in mind-body medicine with such a learned and visionary teacher.

One chilly autumn day as we were completing hospital rounds for his cancer patients, Bernie found a shiny penny on the ground. He told me that finding a penny, particularly face up, was a sign that would come to him at the most synchronous moments. On the face side of the coin are inscribed the words "In God We Trust." "Sometimes it is just a reminder," he told me. At the time, I looked at him very skeptically, trying my best not to be judgmental about his belief in omens and what I considered to be groundless superstition.

After experiencing a more expansive state of mind, I now understand that a communiqué from the Divine may come in the most simple or complex ways. Finding a penny today is always either a needed reminder to keep my faith or a precursor to some positive change. This particular sign might not work for everyone, but it has for me.

Because we are so unique as individuals, we interpret symbols through the filter of our conditioning and personality. We might not always translate the advisements with complete accuracy, but despite this impediment, they can be a priceless form of guidance in our daily life.

Signs, symbols, and syncronicity are not unsubstantiated reverie or figments of the imagination. They are evidence of attempts at communication with us from another dimension that is veiled, mysterious, and difficult for us to comprehend. In that spiritual realm lie forces that want only to help us on our way.

After some time, I was able to identify four methods used for symbolic communication by Universal Mind. The intentional, divine signals used to instruct and tutor us seem to come through:

- Physical objects, such as trees, people, animals, road signs, or stones;

- Synchronous events or "coincidences," such as getting a flat tire, which might have prevented a car accident;

- Numerical symbolism, as all numbers have esoteric meaning; and

- Geometric symbols and universal and cosmic representations of divine ideals, such as the cross and the circle.

Symbols are communicated to each and every one of us all the time, everywhere. They are meant to teach us great and universal truths in simple form.

For reasons I still do not yet fully understand, I had been transported to a magical realm. This world was animated and full of life everywhere I turned, divulging its divinity through camouflaged miracles. I became more determined than ever to pursue the understanding of these new senses. This was a challenge to all the concepts and beliefs I had formerly held, and I was now resolute and steadfast in my goal to embark upon a fervent and diligent quest to discover the true capabilities of the human mind.

This dreamlike reservoir of signs and symbols continued to seep into my psyche, creating an enormous reserve of sage counsel and information.

The more attention I gave to this symbolic language, the more solidly my inner vision evolved. It seemed as if I had previously been sightless and that the marvels of life had been sealed away under layers of conditioning and a shackled mind. Unknowingly, I had been stumbling blindly through life, thinking that we are fundamentally alone in the world, separated, isolated, and divided into billions of meaningless moving parts. But now, I was learning how to "see" for the first time, and what I saw was one, cohesive, unified, and indivisible universe, a ubiquitous cosmos welded together by a transcendental, inconceivable, and infinite intelligence.

Heaven and earth do mutually communicate. We just have to take the time to learn the language of Universal Mind. The next time you feel like someone or something is trying to get your attention or send you a message, be still, listen, and learn.

The profound and enigmatic challenge that I was inescapably driven to pursue—that we are all summoned to undertake—was to learn to generate positive, forward momentum in the process of evolving and refining ourselves to embody love. Love is the destination of the inner journey and the holy grail of all spiritual endeavors, the true measure of inner accomplishment. It is the substance that is eternally generated and transmitted from that other dimension. Love is the ultimate expression and the result of authentic contact with the fragment of God that is within all of us. It is the closest we ever come to our Source and the only true wellspring of joy.

The gauntlet had been thrown. I was the struggling protagonist in this divine drama, and I was anxious to see how it would unfold.

Quantum Leap

> *"In this world of change, naught which comes stays,*
> *and naught which goes is lost."*
>
> —*Swetchine*

t was the fourth day, and this persistent "condition" was not easing. My old, familiar life was fading into the background. My surroundings were now endowed with a nebulous and mystifying quality. The external, physical world was illumined with spiritual light and pregnant with meaning and potential.

Mentally, an entourage of vague yet perceptible transmissions seemed to come at regular intervals like little memos from some anomalous, obscure zone. Part of me longed for a glimpse of anything that was ordinary and routine. In retrospect, this was such erroneous thinking. I was becoming somewhat accustomed to the peculiar sensation of being in a physical body in the physical world, having a mind that was in two dimensions simultaneously and a personality that was putting the brakes on the whole thing! Elaborating further on that dilemma is not possible in words.

The word "dysfunctional" is used so much today that it has become almost threadbare. It means that we repeat the same problem-solving behavior over and over again even though it clearly fails to solve the problem. Most people have a strange tendency to cling in vain to well-known, deeply rooted ideas and patterns despite the fact that they are not working to optimize life and growth. I knew this so well, yet I, too, periodically clenched tightly to my old, worn-out, and hackneyed habits.

I was a reluctant explorer propelled and flung into an uncharted sea without a map or a rudder to guide me. A monumental change was occurring deep within as my perceptions of the world and myself continued to expand far beyond the limitations of the three-dimensional physical reality. A new reality reigned, one that was mysterious, magnificent, magnetic, and magnanimous. My thirst for the truth was unquenchable.

Those first auspicious days were analogous to a near-death experience. I have read that most people return from that experience transformed. Upon being restored to life, they report no fear of death, a renewed faith in God, and a more loving and compassionate nature. A symbolic death was occurring within me—the death of my antiquated thinking and my separated self. Upon the demise of this vintage persona, a spiritual seed was planted. It began to germinate, to burgeon into a tender stalk that was thriving, shooting up and out through dense ground. I could sense a diminutive and delicate budding floret at the crown, strategically extending and reaching for nourishing air and light. The winds that buffeted me were the squalls of fear that both dampened and stirred my spirit.

These early intense experiences were, in actuality, a wake-up call for me. The aftermath spawned a resuscitation and restoration of my true self, which had been dozing and inattentive for so many years. Petty concerns that would normally be of such importance seemed to melt away like an ancient glacier warmed by the heat of the sun. Feelings of compassion began to heal the bruising caused by years of unforgiving intolerance of myself and others.

I call this process of renewal "transmutation," defined as a change into another nature, substance, form, or condition. In biological terms, it signifies the transformation of one species into another. Metaphysically, it is the raising of energy to a new and higher level, a purification process that cleanses away the old and stimulates the new. As a result, the lower energies are uplifted and absorbed into the higher. On a practical and human level, it is the process of bringing personal shortcomings to the surface and transmuting them into realizations of universality.

I was transmuting from a conditioned personality, a person excessively influenced by the surrounding environment, into a child of God. Of course, I was always a child of God. We all are. But our ignorance of this fact makes it extremely difficult to express those divine gifts that are innate in us all. Releasing the layers of stale conditioning that envelops and conceals our spirit allows the essence within us to shine brightly and make manifest our true nature. It allows for emotions to be transmuted into understanding and knowledge into wisdom.

The effect of this transmutation was pervasive. It enabled me to transform ordinary moments into extraordinary events. Friends, family, and community became even more cherished. I learned how to withdraw from the stressful urban pace and be still and open to inner guidance. My obstinate and headstrong temperament was softening; my combative, militant mentality of the 1960s, disarmed.

My existing love of nature was amplified. Animals and trees, always treasured, were now sacred to me. The mere act of looking at a flower was now a profound mystical experience. As I contemplated the flower, I saw within its physical body the Universal Intelligence that created it. I rejoiced and felt reverence upon beholding the vibrant hues that were magnificently blended and chosen for that particular species. It was awe-inspiring to ponder how nature had produced such an electrifying spectrum of shape and color.

Looking even closer, I would examine every satiny, velveteen petal that was eloquently poised, seemingly so pleased with its own beauty. Patiently and wistfully, I watched as the flower unfurled its face to the sun, the plush veneer absorbing the warm, life-giving rays. Its unique fragrance was a sublime gift for the senses, called into existence just to bring joy and pleasure to all who pass by.

All the while, the flower was merely expressing its essence. Similarly, each one of us is a flower in a divine garden. If only we could truly acknowledge our own essence, recognize and fully express our own beauty, and exude our own fragrance.

"Our deepest fear is not that we are inadequate.
Our deepest fear is that we are powerful beyond measure.
It is our light, not our darkness, that frightens us.
We ask ourselves, who am I to be brilliant,
gorgeous, talented, and fabulous?
Actually, who are you not to be?
You are a child of God. Your playing small
doesn't serve the world.
There's nothing enlightened about shrinking so that
other people won't feel insecure around you.
We were born to make manifest the glory of God
that is within us.
It's not just in some of us; it's in everyone.
And as we let our own light shine, we unconsciously
give other people permission to do the same.
As we are liberated from our own fear, our presence
automatically liberates others."
—Marianne Williamson

During these four wondrous days, there were periods of time when I experienced a profound serenity and radiant joyfulness previously unknown to me. Life was transmuted from routine drudgery to an exuberant and magical daily celebration. I had been assisted by divine intervention in moving beyond my formerly narrow perception of myself to viewing all individuals as a minuscule but ever important link in the chain of humanity.

To illustrate this point, I would like to share an experience that took place four years after my walk with Universal Mind. It is a story about transmutation and the metamorphosis that sprung from a great crisis.

It was a steamy day in August and the beginning of hurricane season in Miami when we were hit by the "big one," Hurricane Andrew. The devastation was unimaginable as the city was entirely unprepared for the magnitude of damage to vital services such as potable water and electricity.

Most affected areas were forced to do without these crucial utilities for many weeks. The region that was hit the hardest and referred to as "ground zero" was the small agricultural town of Homestead. Somewhat impoverished before the storm, afterwards, it was unrecognizable.

The trees that were still standing in the aftermath of ferocious, one-hundred-fifty-mile-per-hour winds were stripped of all leaves. They stood grotesquely naked, offering no shade or shelter from the unyielding heat.

The rest were uprooted and had been thrown about like matchsticks. Not one roof was spared, and most homes had been whittled down to cinder block by scattered tornadoes. Only ramshackled gray skeletons of dwellings remained, sprinkled over the desolate landscape. Overturned cars, now not much more than twisted metal, littered the streets. People wandered aimlessly about, either in shock, injured, or in tears. Many lost everything—family heirlooms, security, safety, and shelter.

The city was in chaos; the crisis, immense. But, miraculously, out of this havoc and despair rose the indomitable and boundless nature of the human spirit. Ordinary citizens took to the streets to direct transportation, for no traffic signals nor familiar landmarks remained. Neighbors helped neighbors dig their homes and cars out from under the rubble. Scarce resources such as food and water were shared. The homeless were taken in by strangers. Lost pets were cared for until the owners were found. Goodwill and altruism, the unexpected by-products of the ravaging storm, were widespread and visible everywhere.

The day after the hurricane, I volunteered my services at a school building that had been converted into a makeshift hospital. With limited supplies, the emergency shelter vaguely resembled a mash unit during wartime. Traumatized and wounded people lay on cots everywhere while helicopters whirled about bringing in crucial medicine and water. Even the National Guard were occasionally treated for stress and heat exhaustion. It was bedlam! Pregnant women groaned through their labor pains and gave birth from behind a sheet in a corner of the room. Occasionally, I would hear the wail of a newborn coming into this topsy-turvy world. Compassionate, sympathetic strangers soothed frightened and crying children separated from their parents.

As donations poured in from all over the United States and abroad, hundreds of people volunteered to assist the Red Cross in sorting canned goods and distributing clothing. Gratefully, volunteer physicians and nurses were so plentiful that despite the chaos, everyone received excellent medical care. Many of the doctors put in eighteen-hour days, slept on blankets flung over a concrete sidewalk, and bathed with water pumped from a tanker truck. They sacrificed all comforts so that the wounded could have the few available cots.

I had never witnessed such selfless service and on such a large scale. And all this brutally hard work carried out in ninety-eight-degree weather was wholly for the love of humanity. There was no monetary reward for anyone, no thought for oneself—just a need to help in a time of crisis. Even more amazing was the fact that the majority of volunteers, including the local Red Cross, were now homeless themselves, yet they demonstrated the most tenacious and undaunted altruism and generosity I could have ever imagined. They found room in their hearts to put the needs of others above their own despite the fact that they were swimming in a sea of troubles.

Disasters reveal and make manifest our humanity. So many people had lost everything, yet they were still compelled to help others. I was witnessing our TRUE nature in full expression. Adversity has the power to elevate compassion to the highest rank of virtue. Andrew's savage winds swept away the superficial and the material, exposing the light and love at the core of human nature.

The repercussions from the storm permanently changed the city of Miami. Through calamity and misfortune, the inhabitants of this city were transformed. They became part of a city of cooperation and fellowship in this process of transmutation on a community level.

All who endured Andrew's wrath were reminded by this force of nature of our humanity and interdependence upon one another. This humaneness is within us all the time. Why, then, do we so rarely express it? Do we really need a catastrophe to resuscitate our charitable hearts? Consumerism and materialism have become so ingrained in our culture that perhaps we have lost sight of the fact that we should be driven by sensitivity and concern for others, not by how much we can stockpile and accumulate.

Whether an individual or a city goes through a divine upheaval, the liberation that may occur as a result is quite miraculous. Just what if the two million inhabitants of Miami remained in this mode of service and every day was spent helping neighbors, volunteering, and sharing resources? What prevents us from living this way? Only our restricted minds, closed hearts, and limited perceptions.

Little did I know that the trials and tribulations that I had already endured during my walk with Universal Mind were only just the beginning for me. The intricate effects of my internal dissension could now be clearly seen, and the real work had just begun. The insights I had and the changes I now saw that needed to be made were staggering and encompassed almost every sector of my life. Relationships needed to be improved and deepened, my career would have to be redirected, goals would be reordered, and priorities, realigned. My entire lifestyle would have to be either methodically or abruptly modified and remodeled.

Metaphorically, this was like reconstructing an old, rickety home with the assistance of an architect, my soul. I would have to inspect every room, gut it, rebuild it, and select new colors and furnishings. A large percentage of this home has now been converted, renovated, and rearranged. Because this was a sizable project, it has naturally taken many years to make only the most fundamental repairs. The remainder will be done in slow, gradual steps over the next, oh, forty years or so.

Take a sweeping look at your life right now, focusing first on the external things such as career or marriage. What does not work? What needs to be changed or replenished? Now delve into your internal world. What needs modification there? Do you need to express more patience, kindness, or self-love perhaps?

What prevents you from immediately beginning a self-improvement, personal-growth program that is designed and implemented by you? The evolution and progress of our own souls should be the primary focus of life. What could possibly be more important?

I suspect there are numerous barriers to making personal growth a priority. Of course, we all have our own rationalizations that hold us back and impede our growth. Most of the time, the negative belief systems learned early in life restrict and limit us. Unless we hold a deeply felt conviction and faith that all deities reside within, the strength and motivation to evolve to our personal maximum potential will never be found.

In earlier times, when humanity was not distracted by the endless stream of material possessions that have become so essential to "success" today and money was not traded for vital energy, the attainment of personal growth and spiritual knowledge took precedence. At present, as the millennium nears, spiritual pursuits are pushed into the background or considered irrelevant by far too many.

A sincere desire to change focus requires a deep commitment to cultivating a rich inner life by seeking to learn and grow from every single event that takes place in your day. Sometimes an athlete's stamina and a warrior's spirit are required to accomplish this goal.

Learn to transmute the meaningless into the meaningful, the routine into enchanted realization, mistakes into learning opportunities, and your loneliness into a deep yearning for God. If someone is hostile to you, practice forgiveness rather than reactivity. If you are ill, you may use that time for reflection. Should your car break down, relax; it might enable you to meet someone new. If your spouse abandons you, it just might be time to learn more independence. The possibilities are infinite.

"Make me an instrument of Thy peace;
Where there is hatred, let me sow love;
Where there is injury, pardon;
Where there is doubt, faith;
Where there is despair, hope;
Where there is darkness, light;
and where there is sadness, joy.

Grant that I may not so much seek to be
consoled as to console;
To be understood, as to understand;
To be loved, as to love;
For it is in giving that we receive,
It is in pardoning that we are pardoned;
And it is in dying that we are born to eternal life."
—St. Francis of Assisi

An incident from which I gleaned a major lesson in transmutation occurred during my doctoral internship with Dr. Bernie Siegel. We had met only briefly at a conference when the invitation to train with him was extended. Bernie was not yet well known, and I was not quite sure just what to expect or what was expected of me during my initial stay in New Haven.

I arrived at Yale New Haven hospital with some trepidation on that first day of training. I was prudently dressed in my most professional attire, including two-inch heels. Upon making my way to the designated rendezvous point, I found myself in the outer hallway of the surgical unit and main operating room. Bernie greeted me with a hasty and perfunctory wave of his hand and the grin of a Cheshire cat. "Change into scrubs and meet me in the OR," was his only brief instruction. Seeing the vacant look on my face, an amused, kindly nurse came to my rescue and hurriedly escorted me into the locker room.

I ineptly stripped down to my high heels, pulled on sterile operating room garb, then grappled and sparred with a surgical face mask. I then tucked my long hair into a most unattractive hair net. Feeling rather pleased that at least I had gotten this far and properly clothed, I proceeded into the operating room. The distracting clicking and clunking of my high heels wrapped in sterile shoe covering against the linoleum floor was so comical that I almost lost my professional composure while the patient was being anesthetized.

Twenty minutes into my very first observation of surgery and on this first day of training, the patient went into a sudden crisis from the anesthesia and began to turn blue. As the surgical team began emergency procedures to save his life, my heart pounded, perspiration beaded on my forehead, and disbelief contorted my face into the semblance of a tragic theatrical mask. I made every attempt to camouflage my anxiety, but I was on the verge of panic. I was terrified that this man would die right in front of me.

Standing behind Bernie and several others on the surgical team, I tried to stay out of the way and calm myself. Bernie, his back previously to me, quietly turned away from the patient and said over his shoulder, "It would help more if you prayed."

I closed my eyes, breathed deeply, and not knowing what else to do, began to pray silently with him. At this point in time, I believed neither in the power of prayer nor in a higher intelligence. But pray I did, and it was with colossal, heartfelt conviction because I so wanted this man to live.

The patient survived. I learned an invaluable lesson that I have never forgotten—to transmute a negative situation into a positive and more spiritually focused option. Now, if I am ever afraid, I transmute the fear into prayer. It works every time!

❧ Lessons by the Sea

Later, on the afternoon of the fourth day, I was sitting in my living room, more subdued, and still trying to sort out the real from the unreal.

Making an effort to be as stoic as possible, little by little, I seemed to have acquiesced and yielded a bit to what I still viewed as an aberrant and bizarre state of mind. Even though all the sensations and perceptions were exhilarating, transforming, and constructive, I was intermittently at odds with myself. Two parallel worlds existed, synchronized with one another, harmoniously interactive, and strangely intersecting. They functioned in unison, conjoined by an intelligent, omnipresent force. For some reason, for these few days, I was increasingly in rapport with the more subtle of the two, allowing for fantastic glimpses into a world suffused with knowledge, light, and luminous palettes of color.

A thunderstorm was brewing outside. As the sky darkened and turned a pewter gray and lumbering clouds laden with rain hung ominously in the sky, I sought to comfort myself by cocooning in a fleece blanket and nestling into the coziest chair in the house. Swaddled with the blanket and curled up with a book, a cup of café au lait, and a French pastry, at last, I felt safe and secure, but the fortified bastion I had created was illusory.

Once again, the voice gently intruded, interrupting a much needed moment of tranquility:

"Go to the sea. There you will meet a teacher at 3:00."

An image instantaneously popped into my thoughts. It was a mental picture of a nearby beach at a very specific location. The exact site seemed to have been telepathically projected onto my mind. There was no uncertainty about where I was supposed to go. The real questions were "Am I going to listen to this voice, go out into a rainstorm, and follow instructions from an auditory hallucination?" or "Am I being guided by a divine intelligence and will now go to the beach to meet an important teacher?" Immobilized by this quandary, I could think of only one thing to do. I reached for another eclair.

It was 1:30. I fretfully paced the floor trying to decide between staying and leaving, between sanity and insanity. The relentless interior debates and mental skirmishes created yet another boxing match, the two parts of me sparring for authority. But when I weighed the options and talked to myself about all of the grace and beauty that had adorned my life these last few days, I could only make one choice. With the feud resolved, I found some rain gear and headed for the location that I had visualized.

By the time I arrived at my destination, the thunderstorm had passed, but the weather was still quite blustery and overcast. The beach was completely deserted. Obviously, I was the only one foolhardy enough to be out there on such an inclement and squally afternoon.

Stretching out a quilt over a damp sand dune, I sat down far from the water's edge and sought refuge under the sea grape trees. At first, I enjoyed the idyllic scenery—freighters cruising by like little toy ships on the distant horizon; excitable, flesh-colored land crabs timidly darting in and out of their subterranean homes; and sandpipers scampering about, pressing their long, tapered beaks into the sugary, moist sand. The signature of their trident-shaped footprints engraved the shore like tiny, miniature monograms. It was low tide, and I could see a variety of brightly colored shells strewn like necklaces on the sand, just waiting to be found. I picked up one that glistened gold and white and then another shaped like a dainty violet turban. Positioning them in my palm, I studied the markings that looked like cryptic inscriptions.

In the distance, a blue heron stood in ambush waiting for lunch to swim by. I glanced down at my watch. It was 2:55. "What am I doing here?" I thought, as I started to become uneasy about the decision that I had made. Here I was, perched by the ocean on a stormy day because I had been directed by a voice that told me that I should come to meet a "teacher." I almost expected Yoda from "Star Wars" to come ambling toward me, but I was a solitary figure huddled against the wind on a lone stretch of beach with no one in sight. Feeling more and more ridiculous, I started to think that the whole idea was ludicrous. My eyes brimmed with tears as I groped for composure and hung my head in my hands.

When I looked up, I saw a figure in the distance slowly walking along the shore. My eyes locked onto it and followed every move as it neared. Within a minute or two, I could see that it was a young man, also dressed in foul-weather gear. As he approached, he veered from the shoreline and walked in my direction towards the dunes. My emotions ran the full gamut, like a range of musical scales, before I forced some deep breaths to help me get a grip on my anxiety.

He strolled right up to me and said, "What are you doing out here in this weather?" With limpid eyes, I looked up at him and then, completely mute, glanced down at my watch. It was exactly 3:00.

He was very tall and slightly built, and he had a thick mane of curly black hair. His face had a boyish, almost childlike quality and exuded a youthful charm and allure.

My emotions must have been rather transparent because he then asked, "Are you all right?"

"Not really," was the only reply I could muster. The next question quickly ensued.

"May I sit down?"

Barely in a whisper, I said, "Okay."

His name was Peter. The quilt upon which we sat became a tiny island in a vast savanna of sand. Alone on the beach, we were ironically sequestered by the harsh elements. Before I knew it, I had poured my heart out to him and told him everything — all that had occurred, all of my inner turmoil, and even how I had happened to come to the beach that day. He smiled throughout with loving understanding and shared deep parts of himself about his own struggles with his spiritual faith. I felt an intense and penetrating bond with him, as if we had known each other for eons.

So engrossed was I by his wizardry with words and wit that the hours slipped by unnoticed. The sky had cleared, and the sinking sun provided a dramatic, almost theatrical setting. The burnished backdrop of variegated colors cast a faint glow that shone on his angelic-looking face.

Peter stood up to leave, and after a lengthy, cherished embrace, I watched as he walked away, never looking back. I had not asked him where he was from or where he was going. I did not even know his last name. The few hours that we had spent together had been totally in the present moment, so healing, like salve on a wound. Clearly, it had been preordained that we should meet, two souls out of the billions in the world, connecting on that rainy day, two strangers, brought together by divine guidance for purposes that I could only imagine.

I never saw Peter again, and to this day, I still wonder whether there was more to our meeting than I could comprehend. The lessons that I learned that day by the sea were as numerous as the granules of sand on that beach, but the most salient one is this: We are meant to love one another and to recognize each other for who we really are—divine fragments of the Whole. The simple words "Love our neighbor as ourselves," spoken two thousand years ago, are the key to finding peace on this frenetic planet. With my heart full of love and my head full of wisdom, I came to the profound realization there are no strangers in the world, only potential friends.

II. The Second Walk

Dueling Doctrines

> *"When you eventually see through the veils to how things really are, you will keep saying again and again, this is certainly not like we thought it was."*
>
> —*Rumi*

even months had passed since my first "walk" with Universal Mind. It was now October. The zeal and exhilaration of my experience had long since faded but was still keenly embedded in my memory. I had remained in a supersensory state of awareness for a full week. Even after all these months of reflection, I was still grappling with the actuality of those seven days that had profoundly altered every facet of my being and felt like decades of living and life experience.

From time to time, some part of me would become unyielding and resolute in my denial of the authenticity of what had happened. Doubt would creep into my psyche like an unwelcome shadow. I had been so certain of everything before, so convinced that what I had gone through was real. However, now that some time had passed, I found myself reassessing everything. My old, skeptical mind would periodically resurface and dissect and question every event, every perception. I felt torn, fragmented, and unable to live fully the life that I had so briefly glimpsed.

If my experiences were unequivocally true, the ramifications would be astronomical. I realized that I could no longer maintain a life that held me apart from all other things and people. Curiously, I slightly lamented this potential loss of my personal ego and sense of self-importance. The internal deliberations went on and on. I also knew that it was time to integrate the gifts of inner wisdom with my professional work as a therapist, but I had very little clarity about how to accomplish this.

A powerful polarization between what I had come to know and what I had known frequently left me immobilized and frustrated. I was unable to liberate myself from the conflict. At this point, seven months after my "first walk," one hand was reaching for the doorknob to heaven while the other was securing the deadbolt.

> *"Alas, the world is full of enormous lights and*
> *mysteries, and man shuts them from himself*
> *with one small hand."*
> —Martin Buber

I still occasionally felt that my experiences seemed irrational and illogical. Undoubtedly, I had heard voices, seen visions, and experienced some kind of altered state of consciousness. These sensations are not usually viewed as symptomatic of sanity. But the remainder of the time, my true self, my spirit, triumphed with the unwavering knowledge that other dimensions were waiting to be explored. What a dreadful way to live, being so divided within myself!

Vacillating in a sea of doubt, I decided to consult with the "authorities" in spiritual matters, the clergy who have devoted their lives to their religion and belief in the Divine. I made three appointments. The first was with a rabbi; the second, with a Roman Catholic priest; and the third, with a Lutheran minister.

Walking into a synagogue for the first time in many years brought back pleasant childhood memories. I remembered giggling through services with my friends, but aside from that, this hallowed place of worship with its honeycombed ceiling was just a building. The rabbi who met me at the office door was scholarly looking, bearded, and quite elderly. He fit the stereotype perfectly. With a warm greeting and moving at a snail's pace, he motioned for me to sit down and took his place on the other side of his desk.

With tightly clasped, gnarled hands tactically placed on the massive mahogany desk, the rabbi asked in a fatherly tone, "How can I help you?" "Well, you see, I have been hearing voices, having visions and prophetic dreams, and seeing the silhouette of God. What do you think?"

His eyes widened as he squirmed nervously in his high-backed leather chair. It squeaked as he rocked back and forth trying to collect his thoughts. Looking a bit antsy, he tugged at his coarse white beard and launched into a sermon that was obviously geared to placate me. I sensed that he was wondering if I was so imbalanced that I might present a danger to myself or others. My intuition was correct because in the end, with the best of intentions, he ultimately appealed for me to seek professional help, insisting that no one could know the Divine directly, but only through scripture.

Thanking him for his time, I left a very relieved-looking rabbi in his chambers. A deep loneliness and emptiness overcame me as I walked away. I had just consulted with a revered sage from my own religious background, an individual who has devoted his entire life to religious pursuits, and he did not have the foggiest idea what I was talking about. Would I ever find someone who would understand?

Next on my list was the Roman Catholic priest. In this beautiful church with its soaring, domed ceilings and magnificent stained-glass windows depicting various saints, the exact same scenario unfolded. I left feeling deflated and dejected.

My last resort was the Lutheran minister. This visit involved no theological discussion whatsoever. It resulted in a direct referral to a psychiatrist. At this point, I realized that I was clearly on my own and would just have to find my way and search for the truth by myself.

Ever the scientist, I decided to engage in my own research project to determine just how prevalent higher states of consciousness really were. And so I began a scholarly, systematic search for other people, both in the United States and in Europe, who had had similar experiences. My investigation involved the objective scrutiny and analysis of mountains of writings on the subject. I combed the libraries for detailed accounts of mystical states in the religious scriptures of all the world religions and found, to my delight, hundreds. Interestingly, my search shepherded me not only to religiously oriented writings but also to the biographies and publications of great artists, poets, and musicians.

But what about now, in contemporary times and in the Western world? Was I the only person hearing voices and seeing unusual things who was not mentally ill? I was not, not by a long shot! Happily, I was soon to receive communication and validation from many others who have had life experiences similar to mine, most of whom had kept very quiet about a multitude of profound, transcendental events.

As part of my methodical search, I had placed an ad in a journal devoted to science and spirituality, requesting anecdotal stories of "expanded states of awareness" or "religious and spiritual experiences." The responses poured in! I was inundated with mail, faxes, and phone calls from individuals who wanted to share their diversified experiences.

During the exhaustive task of critiquing each life story and separating fact from fiction, my years of experience in the mental health field and my diagnostic skills were pushed to the limit. However, in the clinical literature, very little information existed that could serve as a foundation for discerning whether the people who had responded had had experiences of mysticism or madness.

A comprehensive library search shed light on the fact that psychiatry has not yet addressed the issue of differentiating between psychopathology and expanded states of awareness. Many of the presenting symptoms of both conditions would look and sound identical to the unenlightened observer.

The current view held by mainstream mental health professionals maintains that mystical experiences are either a form of disassociation—a loss of the usual interrelationship between the various groups of mental processes—or psychosis, the term used to refer to a particular class or group of mental disorders. According to contemporary psychiatry, spiritual realms do not exist, except in the minds of the deranged.

Metaphysical books gave me the sustenance I needed to keep going in the right direction. They were my advocates, inspiration, and source of spiritual nourishment. Eventually, I came across a classic by William James, *The Varieties of Religious Experience*. James, a psychiatrist and philosophy professor at Harvard University in the early twentieth century, conveyed his belief that "religious phenomena, though potentially contaminated with one's own intrapsychic issues, are still religious phenomena." In other words, when someone experiences an expanded state of consciousness, a lifetime of personality conditioning and ingrained belief systems will influence its quality and content.

James began the difficult task of differentiating true religious experience from mental illness or organic disease. At least I now knew that others in my profession were asking the same complex questions and seeking plausible answers. After reading James' book, I gleefully tossed my obsolete Freudian principles out the window. God was not dead for Freud, but very much alive—as a patient! I wanted no part of it!

❧❧❧ What You See Is Not What You Get

I felt disheartened that I was struggling so much when confronted with new perceptions of reality. My lack of preparation for a mystical encounter and propensity toward viewing science and psychology as the only possible ways to interpret unexplained events had failed to give me a suitable vantage point. The consequences of this limited outlook had resulted in a rather traumatic and frightening initial experience and disturbing backlash.

Ever determined to move forward and not slip back into old thinking patterns, I concentrated on being more open-minded in the office and with my work. I soon encountered the perfect opportunity to integrate my new insights in my practice.

A patient was referred to me by a neurologist for stress-related migraine headaches. She had been given every imaginable test, all of which were negative. This lovely young woman proceeded to describe the symptoms.

"Do you have much pain?" I asked.

She responded, "Oh no, I don't have any pain at all. I just experience flashes of bright light before my eyes, and I see geometric symbols."

I continued to probe. "What kind of symbols?"

"Mostly triangles, squares, circles, and a strange shape like two bent lines intersecting each other," she responded.

I went over to my desk and pulled out a chart of universal mystical symbols and pointed to the one she described as two lines intersecting each other. "Is this what you have been seeing?" I asked.

Her eyes widened. "Yes! What on earth is that?"

Medicine and psychiatry view all unexplained symptoms as pathological, or in other words, as "something wrong with the patient." In this case, however, maybe, just maybe, this woman was having brief glimpses into another dimensional realm and she had been told that she was having "migraines" for lack of a better medical explanation.

And what about me? Was everything that I perceived real? Was some of it? None of it? The ruminations continued. Is it really true that there is a God, an immeasurable, boundless, and indeterminate intelligent being that perpetually creates and pervades the universe, an empyreal vital force that is omnipresent in everything? Could it be that we, humanity, are entwined in the body of this being? Is it true that we can communicate with and perceive some aspect of this Supreme Being?

Perhaps I was a bit spiritually learning disabled at the time, but I still could not fully surrender and have faith in that conviction. I was unsure if my mind was a reliable instrument, and my frequent exposure to colleagues who were not open to anything remotely spiritual provided little support. Increasingly, I found myself alienated professionally and very much outside of the dogmatic clan of "rational scientists."

To make matters worse, I had spoken to virtually no one about my experiences because my primary circle of friends and acquaintances worked in the mental healthcare community. Despite our friendship, these well-intentioned professionals would certainly think that I was mad. For them, there was no line of demarcation between madness and mysticism. Mainstream psychology does not consider exceptional states of awareness as an alternative diagnosis.

I had entered into a state of mind that was acknowledged by both my peers and the clergy as illness. Thus, I could never speak of it. I felt divinely abnormal!

> *"Seeing into one's own nature is not the fruit*
> *of study or research.*
> *It is a profound insight derived from living in the heart*
> *of reality, in perfect mindfulness."*
> —Thich Nhat Hanh

In the course of plodding through my reading and studies, I came across a book titled *Many Lives, Many Masters,* written by Dr. Brian Weiss, a psychiatrist at a local hospital. The book chronicles Weiss' clinical and personal impressions involving a patient named Catherine, who recalled past life experiences under hypnosis. Catherine, who was able to act as a conduit for information from highly evolved spirit entities, revealed many of the secrets of life and death to Weiss.

Brian's training, like mine, was quite traditional. He, too, was initially concerned about eliciting an adverse reaction from his peers should he disclose his experiences. In fact, four years elapsed before he was able to write about them. By the time his book was completed, however, he had resolved all conflict and misgivings about publishing it.

This was a person I could totally identify with! He was a psychiatrist, he lived locally, and he had gone through a similar process of introspection and skepticism. But, in contrast, I struggled for seven years before I was able to speak and write about my experiences. Unfortunately, as I have mentioned, I was encumbered by a spiritual learning disability.

Encouraged, I decided to seek professional guidance just once more. Naively and unconsciously, I was seeking validation from a peer that I was not only sane, but ultrasane. Not yet at a point where I had sufficient confidence in myself and in the reality of Universal Mind, I desperately needed to find a compatriot in my field to commiserate with. I soon worked up the courage to call.

My first impression of Brian was a positive one. He seemed to be warm, open, and gentle. His affable and compassionate demeanor allowed me to be immediately comfortable. As my stories and experiences tenuously unfolded before him, he listened attentively. After a long narration of the highlights of my experience, I eagerly and anxiously awaited either positive acknowledgment or cynicism.

I braced as he began to speak, but to my pleasant surprise, his attitude was very nonchalant. He reassuringly said, "Sure, it was real," and then proceeded to tell me one of his own experiences, which he had initially questioned.

This talk with Brian was the catalyst that I needed to help me finally let go of my ambivalence and apprehension and begin to move on. It stimulated a cathartic purging of my self-doubt and mistrust. "It was real!" I thought triumphantly. Someone had said it, someone with an M.D. after his name. Giddy with relief, I also felt like kicking myself because I had needed this confirmation at all. It was sad that my faith was so weak and my courage so lacking that I had to try to legitimize my own perceptions. But at least now I could concentrate on an inward change rather than an outward search. No longer could I resist the pull of spiritual gravity—the magnetic force that is ever guiding us toward the unvarnished truth. I could wholeheartedly continue the journey toward the center of my being.

It is so regrettable that my scientifically oriented training throughout my education fostered a skewed viewpoint which led to a split between science and spirituality. The paradox is that in reality science IS spiritual, and spirituality IS scientific. In fact, the field of psychology initially entailed the study of the soul. "Psyche," which means soul, and "ology," which means the study of, have ancient roots. As the derivation suggests, psychology originated as a religious study. However, through its growth and evolution, psychology eventually took on a more scientific posture and began to concentrate on the body, brain, and biochemical processes. Religion was headed for a collision course with science with the advent of this revolutionary view.

Very slowly, through meditation and the progressive study of esoteric literature, a concept began to take shape in my mind about the nature and composition of our true being and that of our Source. Needless to say, any and all attempts at trying to define or conceptualize the Divine are exceedingly limited given the burden and blessing of a physical body and physical brain. But little by little, a comforting and palatable image began to emerge, one that seemed to me to be both quite logical and even scientifically sound.

The image was not one of a localized, personified deity sitting on a golden throne up in the clouds somewhere, miraculously watching over us at every moment and harshly judging our behavior. This rather childish and one-dimensional view is somewhat analogous to the Santa Claus myth, the enticing fairy tale about a man with a flowing white beard who can simultaneously be all over the world delivering gifts to those who are deserving. Even as a young child, I had thought that the undeveloped and rudimentary concepts of God taught in churches and temples made little sense. This confining and girded doctrine was partially the cause for my rebuffing of organized religion.

Eventually, I spawned the image of an infinite, intelligent, and supreme being that possesses a body, but not in the normal way that we ordinarily visualize a form. This divine body that I perceived is a multidimensional, formless, and amorphous mass composed of an incalculable number of stars and planets, human beings, animals, vegetation, and minerals, all living and flourishing within the realm of this Being. This is an entity whose vital organs are solar systems; whose eyes are pure consciousness; whose blood is circulating, vitalizing chi; whose cells are the living creatures within; and whose pulsating energy released into the universe is the life-giving breath of the Divine. All indwelling matter, ethereal and physical, is governed by certain laws and principles that allow for perfect order, unity, and harmony. This is a being whose eternal and rhythmic heartbeat lies infinitely at the center, timelessly emitting chromatic ripples of unconditional and benevolent Love.

Our own bodies are a microcosm of the Divine. We, in turn, are a composite of living cells, blood, and organs, each component serving a specific function and, under the right conditions, functioning harmoniously. When individual cells are not attuned and in rapport, they may turn malignant, become misguided, and rebel against the entire structure. Running rampant and unchecked, they may eventually destroy the entire organism.

All too often, humankind becomes a muddled, malignant force within this wondrous being by separating, forgetting, and defying the entity within whom we live and breathe. People might maim or massacre a physical part of it only because as Christ said, "They know not what they do." I emphasize the physical part because the spiritual aspect of ourselves and the vital energy that gives us life can never be harmed or extinguished.

Humanity is simply an assortment and collection of individual cells in movement within a vast living organism, their mission being to fulfill their destinies and serve their purpose, just as white blood cells accomplish their life's purpose within our bodies. With time, I came to understand how it is that this feeling of oneness occurs so frequently in stories told since the beginning of recorded history. We can know our Source because we are a miraculous, integral fragment of it. There is literally only One Body, One Mind. Who we really are is simply the result of the cohesive marriage between spirit and matter. Who we intrinsically are is the link between this being we call God and our individual, distinct essence, the connection uniting the perceptible corporeal world and the obscure, imponderable world of spirit.

> *"Matter is spirit at the lowest point*
> *and spirit is matter at its highest."*
> —*H.P. Blavatsky*

Because of my excessively analytical mind, I had been driven by the need for final, irrefutable proof for the existence of God. Of course, Universal Mind will fail the tests that science tries to administer for its own reassurance. But, one thing is sure: It will not fail the test of my own heart. True understanding and faith lies deep within the complicated core of our being. At long last, that was where my search was converging.

The Mystic Marriage

*"Thou art in me and I in Thee, glued together as one
and the self-same thing."*

—*Gerlac Petersen*

So many upheavals had taken place in my life in a relatively short period
of time that it seemed that I had been bouncing on an esoteric
trampoline, tossed high into the air by exalted states and beatific
visions, then awkwardly dropped to the ground by the gravity of my normal
state of awareness. But it seemed that now, almost a year after my mystical
journey had begun, I was finding more balance and poise. This reflected
constructively not only in my personal daily life, but also in my work.

On the 7th of October, I was sponsoring a seminar on "The Joy of
Health" at St. Francis Hospital in Miami Beach. Toward the afternoon of the
second day of the conference, I was fidgety and fatigued from being indoors
for many hours. The crowded, air-conditioned, windowless room, coupled
with the glaring fluorescent lights, was starting to get to me. The lecture
began to feel as irritating and annoying as a dripping faucet. Squirming in
my seat, I had a compelling need, a prodding need, to escape to the comfort
of the sun and fresh air.

The weather was almost too good to be true on this tropical Autumn
day. Since my mind had already been wandering outside for the last hour or
so, I thought I might just as well take my body there too and have all of me
in one place. The ocean was only half a block away, and I knew that a walk

on the beach would rejuvenate me. Succumbing to my nudging impulses, I slipped away from the throngs of people to walk, contemplate, and relax— or so I thought.

Being near the ocean was immediately invigorating, but it also soothed me and gave me solace. As a titillating wind gusted through my hair and blew a humid, salty breeze across my face, I became lost in thought. I rolled up my trousers, took off my shoes, tied my jacket around my waist, and with great abandon, dodged the waves as I strolled down the beach. Continuing to luxuriate in the moment, I stopped, just to ponder life and watch the motion of the water. Rusty-brown-colored pelicans skimmed the rippling surface, effortlessly gliding on unseen air currents. Seagulls screeched overhead looking for a handout.

The warm, inviting surf rolled predictably onto the sand, enthusiastically rushing in and then withdrawing with the same melodious sound. The ocean was alive and breathing, taking long, fluid inhalations as the surf receded. This delicate, soft whispering was followed by forceful exhalations as parades of breakers were heaved willfully to the shore.

Looking out at the east horizon, I let my imagination stretch all the way to Africa. Only the ocean lay between me and that vast continent. The ocean's sweeping boundlessness felt so immense, and I, so inconsequential in comparison. I thought about the potpourri of life underneath the surface of those waves as I remembered a childhood fantasy of longing to be a mermaid and live in the sea. It had always held a great fascination and enigmatic mystique.

When we stand on the shore, we cannot see the thousands of different life forms in their marine environment. What lies below is a magical, brilliantly colored aquatic world that can be accessed only when using the appropriate equipment. Similarly, to pass into divine realms, we must also possess the proper tools to enter, that instrument being a certain state of mind.

While deep in thought and still contemplating the vastness of the sea, the voice unexpectedly returned. It had never occurred to me that it would. I had always hoped but assumed that it was a one-shot deal. This time, I was startled, but not afraid, and considerably more attentive.

"We are sorry that you had to suffer so much pain with your heart."

The voice, which was genderless, had a compassionate and consoling tone. Let me assure you that it did not even vaguely resemble my own thoughts. It was clear and audible, and in the past, it had frequently spoken to me of things that I could not have envisioned in my wildest dreams. For lack of a more deserving name, I started to refer to this voice as my "Mentor."

I knew immediately what the Mentor was alluding to. But who were the "we" it referred to? A gentle, affectionate soliloquy pursued about a very serious, life-threatening illness that I had survived during adolescence. I had suffered repeated episodes of pericarditis, an inflammation of the lining around the heart. The doctors never determined its cause. They treated it symptomatically each time, and eventually it disappeared.

The Mentor cited explanations as to the meaning and purpose for the physical suffering that accompanies any illness. My response was a subdued and stupefied "Really?" I was surprised by this information in particular because this illness had happened so long ago, and although it was very devastating at the time, I did not think about it very often. I could not comprehend why the topic of physical suffering had been brought up at all, but within months I would understand the importance these words would play in my life.

Again, as before, there was a didactic quality to the discussion. I thought that perhaps some ethereal being or beings were trying to help me in a very profound and personal way. But who or what? Was it my higher self? A guardian angel? A collective consciousness? God? No clear answers were forthcoming, but I had an impeccable faith that the experience was very real and the voice was definitely speaking to me from some higher, ubiquitous realm.

The Mentor explained that the causes of illness are not always clear. Sometimes sickness can have metaphysical origins caused by great pressure on the body from subtle, awakening energies. Illness can also be nature's benevolent way of encouraging movement and growth. There can be tremendous dissension from the torrents of inflowing energy and shifting forces that happen to all of us during our life cycle. The transmutation process that inevitably occurs, elevating the lower energy to the higher, can potentially stress the body to the point of illness. These divine physical upheavals are part of the evolutionary process itself. Most of the time, we are not aware that these disruptions in the status quo are serving a very important function. Human life, the Mentor explained to me, is the evolutionary gateway through which the true self can enter the realm of all things divine.

Disease can be both an emancipating stimulus with the potential to reorganize that which is stagnant and the by-product of the metaphysical developmental process. The Mentor reminded me that disease is found in all the four kingdoms of nature. Every living thing is constantly changing, continually evolving, and periodically, this sacred prodding can wound a bit.

Throughout its entirety, the exchange between us was entirely telepathic. The transmission of thought was like the reception of radio waves—invisible, yet tangible. I was more keenly aware than ever before that the greatest reality is that which you cannot see. Although there were dozens of people around me as I walked, I was oblivious to them. I listened vigilantly as the Mentor continued.

The Mentor proceeded on to a discussion about "distraction" and pointed out my difficulty in staying focused and keeping my mind "steady in the light." Specifically, the Mentor was helping me to understand how I frequently became diverted from my spiritual path. This was certainly nothing new to me but still very illuminating and even comforting. It is the very common experience of knowing the "right" thing to do in any given situation and then not doing it. Such a peculiar tendency we all have.

We walked and talked together for some time. A chat ensued on many matters—the universal laws, the concept of one world religion, money as a potential expression of divinity and love, inner training, immortality, service to others, and practicing harmlessness.

Though the Mentor made no allusions to impending cataclysms, for some reason I suddenly became concerned about radical changes and upheavals that might occur on the earth at the time of the new millennium. I perceived a great and pressing need for all of us to begin to shift our focus from material concerns to spiritual pursuits. I instinctively felt very troubled about the future of the environment and the direction that humanity has taken.

Numerous trends indicate that the technological era is engaged in a dire battle with nature. Unless we begin to change our priorities from being outwardly wealthy to inwardly abundant, we risk the destruction of our beautiful planet and, ultimately, ourselves. We need to make a conscious and concerted effort to reorganize our lives so that we function and coexist harmoniously with all of nature and each other. I had a resounding sense that I was being drafted to assist in preparing myself and others for these changes that might occur, or better yet, to do my small part in helping to prevent them.

The knowledge transmitted to me at this time was utterly foreign. Concepts such as the continuity of life as a soul had to be patiently explained. The Mentor introduced the idea that our life cycle is not limited to the period of time between birth and death. Rather, it is an infinite process as our true selves, our souls, continue the rebirth experience. Each lifetime is an opportunity to learn and develop divine traits until the body no longer holds the spirit prisoner but uses it as an ideal channel to express itself. This current life is but one fraction of a sequence of experiences that will eventually lead to the soul's ultimate goal, realizing itself.

Each lifetime, including the present one, is so terribly important to the soul's journey and to humanity's pilgrimage because every spirit has a specific mission to fulfill. We choose to come to the physical world to complete that mission. We all have a destiny, and that destiny is to BE—to be our essence, not our personalities; to be our spirit, not our conditioning. All of life is meant to be an individually designed, original, yet archetypal odyssey that is for the "soul" purpose of evolution.

> *"The human soul is like a bird that is born in a cage.*
> *Nothing can deprive it of its natural longings,*
> *or obliterate the mysterious remembrance of its heritage."*
> —Epes Sargent

Everything we do in our lifetime, whether positive or negative, impacts both our own spiritual development and that of humanity. We do not live in a vacuum. On a metaphysical level, everything is connected and affects everything else. The old saying "If you pick a flower, you disturb a star" is literally true. Physicists now refer to this as the "butterfly effect." They believe it is factual that when a butterfly beats its wings, a storm may begin across the world.

The Winds of Grace

The Mentor was quiet for several minutes. I continued to meander along the shore enjoying the cool, wet sand under my bare feet. I looked back at my footprints, which were quickly washed away by the surging breakers, and was reminded of the fleeting impermanence of each life.

Then, again, the Mentor spoke. The tone of the voice had shifted slightly. Once again, came an instruction, or rather, an assignment:

"You will soon find a heart-shaped stone."

Meticulously, I studied the sand as I walked, looking for this object and assuming that I was supposed to pick it up when found. Perhaps a minute later and fifty yards down the beach, sure enough, there was the stone. It was a perfectly shaped heart, rather flat, smooth to the touch, and bleached almost white by the sun. It looked like it had been tumbled by the sea for years, gingerly shaped by a loving, invisible hand, and then tossed with great intent onto the shore. I was not the least bit surprised to find it.

I stooped down and ceremoniously picked it up. It was like a rare and precious jewel in the palm of my hand. I examined and inspected every inch of it, all the while filled with reverence for this gift. It was a glorious offering from the sea, a cosmic present, given with Love.

I was clutching the stone in my hands when the Mentor began again:

*"This stone represents your heart. The sand on it, symbolic of
the impurities. Throw the stone into the ocean which is God.
The impurities of your heart will be washed away."*

Tears trickled from my eyes. The saline droplets mingled with the saltwater. An oceanic sensation swept over me as I flung the stone as far as I could and watched as it was quickly swallowed by the waves.

Instantaneously, I was united with the Creator of All with my mind, my soul, and my heart. It was a silent marriage vow, a sacramental ceremony to mark a rite of passage into spiritual life. My maid of honor was the sun; the seagulls, my witnesses. This sacred rite was unknowingly attended by many others on the beach who were no longer strangers, but family, children of God, and a part of myself. It was a grand marriage, a true union of my spirit with All.

In the sand, right where I was standing, someone had drawn two circles intersecting each other. Separate, but one, these became my rings, joining me inviolably with my Source. A higher form of consciousness had been struggling for supremacy, and finally, I surrendered. Together, the ocean and I took long, deep breaths.

In accordance with two old Zen sayings—"Teachers might open the door, but you must enter yourself" and "Before a man can tread the path, he must become the path itself"—I had entered willingly onto this path and into this mystic marriage, and my spiritual self had awakened. The only proper finale to love is union—a lifelong and eternal bond that can never be broken.

An invulnerable serenity and freedom filled me as a gentle breeze carried me along the shore. I looked up to realize that I had walked three miles down the beach. I had been so completely absorbed in this experience that I lost track of time. For that instant, there was no time, only the moment.

All around me, children played, boom boxes blasted, and tanned bodies bobbed in the surf. For everyone else, it was just a normal day at the beach. Overflowing and brimming with joy, I mentally spoke to the Mentor, wanting to wax eloquently about the experience. There was no response, only my own thoughts. With a knowing smile, I knew that the Mentor had gone away, though not very far.

Under the Monk's Wing

"If we do not develop within ourselves this deeply rooted feeling that there is something higher than ourselves, we shall never find the strength to evolve to something higher."
—Rudolf Steiner

n the esoteric literature it is said that "When a student is ready, a teacher appears." A spiritual coach was about to enter my life, an event that could only have been an act of grace, an intercessory blessing from the higher realms. This tutor would eventually nurture and nourish the metamorphosis that was occurring and provide the alchemy needed to help transmute my life from base metal into gold.

Now convinced of the validity of my experiences and the existence of spiritual realms and entities, I was still not comfortable talking about them. With the exception of Peter, I had remained silent for fear that in the course of sharing my insights I would be leaving myself open to misinterpretations and harsh judgments. The sanctity of the experiences needed to be preserved, and I was not sure that discussing them would accomplish that. But the time now seemed ripe for me to emerge from the secrecy and begin to test the waters of public opinion.

I chose to begin cautiously with someone very philosophical and trustworthy, one of my older sisters, Andy. She had lived in Santa Fe, New Mexico for many years, teaching and studying the indigenous dance of the Southwest Native American culture. Peacefully coexisting and interwoven with the Indian way of life there is a large New Age community. Both groups are infused with spiritual-mindedness and a sage respect for the environment. Most residents successfully straddle the two cultures. I felt confident that she would be open to this sort of thing.

It was a good first choice. As I related the whole story to her, she became quite animated and excited. She certainly did not look at me as if I were crazy, which was a concern that I had not yet conquered. I still battled the sinking feeling that I was the only one that understood its actuality. That was far from the truth.

After listening intently, Andy began an impassioned, academic plea for me to seek counsel from someone who might be able to intercede and help to accelerate the understanding and integration of the whole ordeal more thoroughly. Without missing a beat, she quickly arranged for us to meet with an East Indian monk, born in Bombay, who was then living at a retreat center in Oklahoma. They had met in Santa Fe years before. She zealously described him as a remarkable and exceptionally evolved person. Not particularly enthusiastic, I expressed my usual skepticism.

Thankfully, my sister does not easily take "no" for an answer when she feels adamant about something. Before I even had an adequate chance to protest, we were both thirty thousand feet up in the air and flying to the small Midwestern town of Coyle, a remote farming community barely on the map. To this day, I have no idea what provoked this decision or why I went. All I know is that it was destined to be and life-altering.

We landed in Oklahoma City, rented a car, and began the ninety-minute drive to Coyle. The landscape that whizzed by the car window was somewhat monotonous, bare, dry, and flat in extreme contrast to the tropical climate I was accustomed to. It seemed parched and thirsty for moisture. Massive expanses of rural farmland were dotted with barns, silos, and cattle. Bales of golden hay were stacked in calculated geometric piles forming an intriguing organic architecture.

As Andy drove, I stretched back in the seat and surrendered to the hypnotic lure of the isolated stretch of straight road ahead. Arriving at our destination, we turned off the main street onto a dusty dirt road and saw a sign that read "St. Francis of the Woods." By then, I was fairly adept at listening to the mysterious language of the universe communicating through signs, symbols, and syncronicity and was immediately struck by the synergy of the name.

As I exited the car, I found myself standing on land named after St. Francis of Assisi. Something clicked in my mind, and I started putting together some interesting "coincidences." For the first time, I recognized that I had been born in St. Francis Hospital, I had been hosting a conference at that same St. Francis hospital on the day of my "second walk," St. Francis and I shared the same birthday, and I was now at St. Francis of the Woods. Even with my spiritual learning disability, I was bowled over by the paralleling serendipity. I did not have even the foggiest notion what all these coincidences meant to a Jewish girl from Miami. What possible connection could I have to a thirteenth-century Italian saint? I was totally clueless, but I had learned that EVERYTHING has meaning, so I just assumed that it did. I was sure of one thing—that even if I failed to grasp its significance immediately, it would definitely come to me later.

We were soon greeted by an engaging, white-haired man in his sixties whom Andy introduced as Dr. Shyam. I could only describe him at that moment as, well, downright jolly. He had a sensational smile and a stunning and dignified presence. There was something immediately jarring about being in his company, but certainly not in a negative way. He exuded an alluring, magnetic quality and an inexplicable charisma even though his demeanor was subdued and composed.

As he graciously showed us to our bungalow, the polished and cultured manners of his British influence were clearly visible, although his speech was thick with his native Indian accent. We were cordially invited to join him for dinner, and then he sprinted away with the energy and agility of a much younger man. He quickly disappeared through the trees eagerly followed by two huge, frolicking dogs.

It was nightfall and only faint light remained as we walked the quarter mile to Shyam's home. The sprawling landscape was tranquil and still, so unlike the constant, noisy drone of the city. I could almost hear the silence in between an occasional cricket song. As the sky darkened, the constellations became fully visible and diligently flickered against a perennial blanket of indigo. It looked as if someone had repeatedly pierced the opaque fabric of the sky with tiny pinholes, allowing the light behind to shine through. It was so beautiful and very peaceful.

Shyam was diligently preparing dinner, and, of course, Andy and I volunteered to assist. The mundane act of cooking dinner that night was the beginning of years of intensive training with this captivating man on life and its paradoxes, the grandeur of love, spirit and its expansion, and consciousness and its culmination in the divine, just a few of the many topics we have discussed and debated over the years. In my earnest search to find the remote pieces of the puzzle that can decipher the mysterious workings of the universe, this trip was the inaugural event.

Andy and I were assigned the simple task of chopping vegetables, but even that routine act soon turned into an exercise in the ancient tradition of Ayurveda, "the science of life," a practice of Indian medicine over four thousand years old. Shyam explained to us that the primary use of Ayurveda is the medicinal application of plants and food for healing, though it is certainly not limited to that. We were reminded that within the most ordinary vegetation and minerals are potent, life-enhancing medicines to treat almost any ailment that could befall humanity. As Shyam continued his discourse on nature and how it perfectly and intentionally provides us with absolutely everything that we need, I began to understand why it is so essential to preserve it.

This seemingly ordinary dinner was an indoctrination on the importance and interconnectedness of the dominion of animals, plants, and minerals. He went on to explain that all kingdoms in nature have a vitality, purpose, and unique level of consciousness.

"Even minerals have latent within them enormous power," he patiently explained. "As an example, uranium has long been used for atomic energy and quartz crystals were originally utilized as a conductor for radio waves. Intrinsically, both have profound hidden forces concealed within their components. We have only just begun to tap the possibilities. The potent essence and energy of the minerals are absorbed and utilized by the plant world. Energy is actually the living activity of the spiritual realm. Continuing the cooperative effort, the vegetation also receives its sustenance from the energy in the sun and water. So, when we eat an apple from a tree, we are receiving the innermost essence of the minerals, sun, water, and the plant itself. The casual act of eating a piece of fruit should be a sacred rite, the ingestion of the vitalizing and life-giving elements of nature. The ritual of prayers at mealtime developed long ago as a way of expressing gratitude for this miraculous coordination of natural forces."

The dinner preparations were also a unique experience. I had never seen anyone handle food with such reverence and precision. The medicinal properties and effect of each spice on the body became the topic of a lengthy and eloquent dissertation. While gently stripping the onions of their skin, Shyam took advantage of the moment by using the onion as an example of a metaphor for life. "Many layers, many lives, many realities," he quipped. Frequently, he would throw out cryptic remarks and then move on to another subject. His unconventional style of conversing was engaging and playful, yet always pragmatic.

Shyam proceeded to explain how energy follows thought and how our thoughts and intentions affect the food's quality. I was reminded of the Mexican film "Like Water for Chocolate," in which the food prepared by the heroine becomes saturated with whatever emotion she was feeling at the time. Those who ate her food were imbued with those same emotions and impulses. It is a very hilarious film with a plot that has some element of truth.

The result of our combined culinary efforts was a saffron-scented feast that was undeniably the best meal I had ever had. As we ate, Shyam began a discussion about consciousness at the atomic level.

"Every atom in your body is a submicroscopic electromagnetic device. The atom itself is a self-contained unit of energy distinctly separate from the others, but functioning harmoniously and collectively. It, in turn, is made up of innumerable revolving electrons. There is an absolute intelligence or psyche, if you will, within this electric force of nature. The atom is a living entity and possesses a certain level of consciousness. Our bodies are composed of these atoms. A human being is just a gathering, a conglomeration of these conscious particles. They intelligently accumulate to build forms according to a plan. That plan is only known to the master builder, the Divine Architect."

He was confirming what I already knew—that science and spirituality were not separate, but are one and the same. If we could perceive spirituality as science and science as spirituality, perhaps this concept would be more easily embraced and digested by those who have a difficult time with intangible ideas and beliefs. I certainly was not exempt from that dilemma. The discussion was riveting. Though I had a million questions to ask, I just listened.

As we drank English tea and gorged ourselves with homemade rice pudding, Shyam continued, "There is an old Sanskrit saying, 'Know thyself, for in thyself is to be found all that there is to be known.' If you perceive each human being as a collection of intelligent atoms, that person is really an assemblage of consciousness. If you extend the idea a little further and consider a planet as a convergence of atoms and all forms of life on it a coherent whole, then the planet itself is a conscious entity. Keep going with this thought and think of the solar system in the same way. In the heart of the solar system is the sun, the nucleus of energy around which all the planets revolve, omnipotently held in orbit by some phenomenal law of nature. So, you see, an atom is really identical to a solar system, and it is all made up of the same substance of the universe—consciousness and energy."

Andy and I were mesmerized by the discussion. We sat and talked until late into the night. When we could no longer fend off the drowsiness, we finally retired.

More Questions, More Answers

The next morning, I bounced out of bed ready for more. After breakfast, we all took a long walk. The retreat was built on four hundred acres of land, and it supported itself by doubling as a working farm. We meandered down a labyrinth of long, winding paths through waist-high grass and cornfields, occasionally spotting small chipmunks and rabbits as they scurried away through the underbrush.

In an instant, I again experienced the same expansive state of mind as I had before. I turned to Shyam to discuss it with him and unfurled the whole mind-boggling story of what had occurred at home. He looked at me with the cunning of a lynx and began to explain what had happened to me then and what was happening now.

"You became suddenly conscious and saw beyond the facade of things," he said. "Through the ages, when people have claimed to 'see' or 'hear' God, all that has happened is that they momentarily glimpsed through the illusion that everything is separate. They peeked straight into the substance of things and saw the indivisible totality. You experienced this as a moment of crisis because of your narrow, parochial thinking and antiquated psychological training. If you are not prepared for it, the experience can be quite bewildering and frightening. Sometimes, people actually do have periods of very severe stress because the strain of seeing Reality is so great. The event is usually called 'illumination' because all knowledge and wisdom is a form of light. This beacon of awareness reveals things previously unknown and is quite destabilizing. When you open the door directly into the Universal Essence, into your own self which is a fragment of it, you can no longer be satisfied with your old way of life."

"Our universe is multidimensional, not the one-dimensional world that we perceive with our five senses," he explained. "Achieving direct contact with the segment of the Divine that resides within you allows for 'soul senses' to come into play and enables your consciousness to be in close proximity with the fourth and fifth dimensions. Some time in the future, all of humanity will develop clairaudient and clairvoyant abilities, the capacity to hear and see as clearly on the more subtle planes of existence as in the physical."

"Can you elaborate on that a little more?" I queried. "I'm a bit lost."

"Certainly. I can only try to describe fourth-dimensional perceptions as a shift away from linear thinking and being able to 'see' through and around things. It is perceiving from a three-hundred-sixty-degree angle, sort of like having eyes in the back of your head. In that dimension, there is no straight time line as we have come to know it. The past, present, and future can be perceived all at once."

"Fifth-dimensional perception is the capacity to be in full rapport with all that exists," he said. "There is no separation. This level of consciousness enables the person to truly see that there is only One Body, only One Mind. It is sort of like a direct experience of seeing through the eyes of another person or animal. When you delve more deeply into it, you can even perceive through the consciousness of plants."

I was perplexed and slipped back into my clinical mode. "That sounds very much like a form of psychosis," I retorted. "What is the difference then between madness and mysticism?"

His voice instantly took on a more sober tone. "Oh, there is a great chasm between the two. Insanity can have a strictly organic cause, such as a brain disorder, or it can be caused by a rapid inflow of cosmic force that the person is not equipped to handle physically. The deluge can then cause a chemical imbalance. In complete contrast, mystical experience is utter sanity. There is one more cause of insanity that was recognized in ancient times, but only now in certain cultures. It is true that there are cases of possession by misguided discarnate people and probably is the source of most diagnosed multiple personality disorders. Emotional trauma can be a predisposing factor in susceptibility."

I desperately wanted to understand. It seemed that most of what I had been taught during my formal education had just scratched the surface. Basically, I had been trained to believe that psychological troubles arose either because our parents were limited, or there was a biochemical imbalance. Now I had to factor the metaphysical into the equation. I tried to ask more questions, but Shyam changed the subject. I have learned over the many years of our friendship that everything he does has a purpose and an intention. We moved on to rather humorous and frivolous storytelling.

We had walked miles around a perimeter of flourishing, gilded wheat fields when Shyam began telling the epic saga of his own life. He told of many adventures in India, and how, at the age of fourteen, he became a celibate monk of his own volition and maintains that personal commitment to this day. Twelve years were spent in the Himalayas studying and practicing a monastic life, and although he was from an affluent Brahmin family, he renounced all material wealth.

My favorite story was the one that he tells with great joviality. For almost a year, Shyam had lived completely alone in a cave located on the top of a mountain range. He called this cavern home even though there were no conveniences and no companionship except for the hospitality of a family of bears. He told us tales about the eventual acceptance by the bears of this odd coexistence and of their untamed, yet compassionate nature. After some months, when the bears would return from foraging in the woods, they would actually leave food for him, and man and beast lived side by side, peacefully and harmoniously. There was so much I could learn from Shyam, and for some reason, he wanted to teach me.

The complex and beguiling story of his life was so fascinating that it sounded almost fictitious. I was spellbound by this man and found his wisdom, poise, and presence of mind enthralling. He seemingly had his finger on the universal pulse and an internal modem directly wired to the cosmic computer.

He answered every question I could throw at him, and each response was more profound than the prior one.

Weary from walking so far, we headed back via a different route. This one took us past rustic farmhouses and scenic ponds. A pair of graceful opaline swans fluidly glided through a sheath of pea-green water in a superbly choreographed duet. The water was clear enough to see large, spotted fish ambling beneath the surface. Flawless violet lilies with broad, glossy leaves floated with nobility, their roots reaching down into the inky mud. Another metaphor, courtesy of nature. A misty haze draped the pond and gave the whole area a dreamlike effect. I changed my original perception of Oklahoma. It had its own distinctive brand of beauty.

At lunchtime, we again joined in the ritualistic food preparation. I was developing great chopping proficiency, placing each fragrant herb in small sequential piles. As we slid the vegetables into a pot, I just had to ask the most pressing question of all, "Who or what had communicated with me months before?"

Shyam did not look up. He was intensely concentrating on just the right combination of herbs, spices, and multicolored vegetables for his culinary masterpiece, a Brahmin Indian stew.

A minute passed before he spoke. "Did you know that each color in the vegetables has a very specific effect on people?" he asked.

Not knowing why he was being evasive, I repeated my question.

After a very long pause he began, "There is a community of souls, a network of spiritual energy, people, if you will, that have, through their millennia of lives, undergone such an expansion of consciousness that they now function strictly on the spiritual plane. They have reached a point in evolution where they have triumphed over matter and no longer reside in the dense physical world. They ARE in physical existence, just not like you and I. Their bodies are much more refined and immaterial. They have evolved to a level of consciousness that is strictly mental and where communication is telepathic, both with each other and with those living on the earth."

"They are, in effect, the intermediaries between us and the Creator of All. We, in turn, are the midway point between the subhuman and superhuman realms. Their only purpose is to be of service and function as advocates for us. Humanity's mission is to function as an advocate for all living things," he explained, as he tended to the pots on the stove. "Throughout history, they have been called angels and pictured in art as celestial beings graced with glowing halos and feathered wings. This is just a limited view. They are spiritual ambassadors whose profound intent is to assist our souls in the evolutionary process, expedite consciousness, and transmit the will of God."

My breathing quickened. "Why me? Why did they speak to me? I wasn't a religious person," I stammered.

Shyam's answers were calculated and deliberate. "They are communicating with everyone all the time, but in many different ways. Why they spoke to you directly is for you to figure out. It is all so mysterious and grand," he said with his usual intoxicating laughter.

The days timelessly melted into each other. We soaked up all the information our tired minds could grasp. When the moment came to return home, we sadly and reluctantly said our goodbyes to Shyam and headed for the airport.

Sliding my seat back on the plane, I felt gratitude for the astounding events that were constantly unfolding and gave thanks for the many extraordinary and beloved people in my life, both the familiar and the new. Andy and I talked endlessly about the comforting and staggering recognition that there really are loving ethereal beings in constant rapport with us and available to help at all times. It was a life-changing and heartening realization for both of us.

Outside the window, chalk-white, pillowy clouds piously drifted through a sapphire-blue sky. The last few days had soothed my spirit and nurtured my heart. I did not need to be way up in the clouds to be close to heaven; I just had to close my eyes. Given the miraculous adventure I had been on, what could possibly be next?

III. The Night and Dawn of the Eclipse

Arrival of the Shadow

> *"The gem cannot be polished without friction, nor man perfected without trials."*
>
> —Chinese Proverb

I did not know it at the time, but the next turbulent miles of my spiritual expedition had been foretold by the Mentor in those seven words spoken to me at sunset, "Keep the light, even in the darkness." I am grateful that I did not then understand those words nor connect that message with an actual event. But the guidance given was the buoy that kept me afloat through the cavernous abyss that I would soon be forced to navigate.

Had I known what was to come, that foreknowledge would have certainly derailed my steady, disciplined trajectory toward continued spiritual growth and development. I might have spiraled down out of a weightless orbit into a crash-and-burn landing. The Mentor had the wisdom to give information to me only at the right time and only in ways that I could slowly digest.

There is an abundance of time-worn stories about the afflictions and adversities of humanity and the profound wisdom and understanding that might spring from that suffering. Though mine is a contemporary tale, it is a saga that reflects an age-old journey from the darkness to the light.

Six months had passed since meeting Shyam, and my life could not have been more perfectly balanced. We remained in close contact, and he continued to masterfully guide and tutor me in every conceivable esoteric discipline. I no longer felt adrift at sea nor sought refuge in dark corners, alone with my "secret life."

Worlds of opportunity, both professionally and personally, beckoned and incredulously flung open golden doors for my exploration. I was working hard and traveling extensively. At last, the positive repercussions of all that had happened were beginning to mold and shape my obstinate and wayward personality into a more compassionate, cooperative, and forgiving human being. I was more open to the creative energy dwelling inside me and had begun to explore new artistic hobbies and diverse interests.

Never before in all my forty years had I experienced any prolonged periods of peace of mind. Now, tranquillity and inner balance felt like the normal and natural way to be. The familiar and skin-deep restlessness and angst were gone. More importantly, daily life, regardless of where I was and what I was doing, was spiritually focused.

I seemed to have developed a binary awareness, a sense that my consciousness was focused on both the physical world and in the spiritual realm simultaneously. This new aptitude and point of concentration continually brought sacred meaning to the most mundane of activities. Even simple tasks such as grocery shopping or driving became sources for great happiness as I saw spirit within people and nature.

The lessons that I had learned by the sea enabled me to feel that all of humanity was related, and so I began to talk to "strangers" everywhere I went. People always cheerfully responded, happy to have brief contact with a smiling face. These chance meetings usually left me feeling filled to the brim and overflowing with prosperity. I was thoroughly enjoying a newborn sense of community and connectedness. The world was now a friendly place, filled with hope, dreams, and possibilities. I felt invincible and incredibly blessed.

However, Universal Mind and my own individual fate (or "karma" as it is called in India) had a profound and potent lesson awaiting me. The long-elusive serenity that I had finally cultivated was not to continue for long. A normal life was not destined to be for seven long, wretched, and agonizing years.

It was at this time that an ordinary but virulent flu-like illness forced me into bed for a few days. Of course, I thought nothing of this very normal life event. I passed the time reading and watching videos, waiting for this "virus" to make an exit so that I could return to my very hectic and rather demanding work schedule. I was annoyed at the intrusion of sickness and eagerly calculated the number of days it would be before I could resume dance classes and my exercise regimen at the gym.

As the days passed, the illness that had eerily gripped me did not subside, but worsened. It seemed as if this virus had sailed into port, dropped anchor, and disembarked. I grew weaker with each passing day and soon could barely walk unassisted. When I did make the effort to get up, my gait was glacial, sluggish, and tortoise-like.

Unable to eat, I rapidly dropped weight off a body that had once been healthy and fit. A vacant, holocaust-like expression peered out from ashen skin. I did not recognize the unfamiliar face in the bathroom mirror. I looked and felt like I was dying. To add insult to injury, severe and unrelenting pain decided to join its uninvited companion, fatigue. Each day was a living nightmare.

Within months, I had run the gauntlet of specialists in every conceivable field of medicine—neurology, rheumatology, endocrinology, and many others with unpronounceable names. One after another, they stroked their chins in that maddening classic gesture and confessed that this was, indeed, quite a problematic and baffling medical problem. What they found so "medically fascinating" was pulverizing my life into worthless dust.

The same scenario unfolded in each succeeding doctor's office. A shrug, prescriptions for toxic pharmaceuticals arbitrarily written to treat an unidentified malady, and a remediless prognosis. I was told that I had developed an "atypical immunological disorder of unknown etiology" and that it was absolutely incurable. The doctors were handing me a life sentence with no chance of parole. It seemed that my plight was getting more hopeless, and the anguish, both physical and emotional, increasingly more grievous and relentless.

There were no answers nor aid coming from traditional mainstream medicine, no knight in shining armor galloping to my rescue. I was on my own, lambasted and mauled by this plague that had maliciously sutured itself into the marrow of my being. I had never felt more alone in my life despite the outpouring of support from family and friends. I was now an innocuous invalid, an ailing and debilitated shell of my former self, for reasons unknown. Once so filled with divine grace and vision, why was I now plunged into this dark grotto? Just as my life was peaking, brimming with meaning and purpose, I had plummeted headlong into an abysmal pit. The blessings that I had received in the recent past were not something that I ever consciously sought, nor was this.

I pleaded with the Mentor to help, to speak with me. There was only a deafening silence, a mute void, and a painful feeling of utter alienation from everything.

With the passing months, I became more fragile and enervated by the sedentary and almost vegetative lifestyle. A bird-like frailty now graced my thin frame, making efforts at many ordinary physical acts useless, like pouring water through a sieve. I did not have the stamina nor the strength to stand for long and was usually too weak to even talk, thus discouraging most social visits. The simple act of showering usually sapped my energy for the day.

The gnawing pain assaulting my muscles and joints left me frequently writhing in agony, making it impossible to concentrate long enough to even read. Bizarre neurological symptoms affected my memory and ability to concentrate. It was a common occurrence to struggle feebly out of bed to retrieve something, only to forget the task the moment I was on my feet. I would slump back to bed in hushed, lethargic frustration. Impotent pellets of tears frequently oozed from downcast eyes, beading into pallid, glassy droplets on my cheeks.

As more months perished with no change in my condition, the oppressive burden upon my family became crushing to me. I made the decision to hire a full-time aide to give them all a much needed emancipation and respite from my woes and desolation. But it was I who truly needed deliverance—liberation from my gloom and torment. I prayed ceaselessly.

Letting Go

At this stage of this catastrophic and obscure malady, I was forced to make a wrenching decision and abandon my once-thriving private practice, resign a faculty position at the university medical school, and abdicate my memberships at the gym and dance studio. My health was gone, and it was not getting better. My thoughts were tumbling into morose and perilous places. A sinister darkness encased me, its walls so thick they were impenetrable. One of the cosmic jokes that I can now look back upon with some humor is that prior to this affliction I had founded and developed a large wellness center for the treatment of chronic and catastrophic illness. The philosophy of the center was founded on the concept of self-healing and hope. I desperately struggled to muster up both.

Years of training with Bernie Seigel and other notables in the field had helped me gain the reputation as an "expert" in psychoneuroimmunology, the study of mind-body medicine. Patients had flown in from all over the United States and the Caribbean to seek my counsel. The center was at its peak of productivity and success when my life fractured into pieces, and eventually, it had to be shut down. Now I had the opportunity to practice what I had been preaching. The irony was perfect.

Steadily and methodically, all that I had worked so hard for and built up had collapsed. The process reminded me of an exercise taught to Zen monks centuries ago as part of their spiritual training. They were required to build a house from the foundation up—stone by stone, painstakingly by hand—only to disassemble it upon completion, one stone at a time, in deep contemplation and silence. This exercise is meant to be practice in the art of non-attachment to the physical world.

A similar exercise practiced by Buddhist monks today involves the creation of massive "mandalas," or wheels of life, through the art of sand painting. These sacred images sometimes take hundreds of hours of painstaking work to complete, only to be ceremoniously destroyed in an instant.

I did not realize just how attached I was to these things that I was losing and how much they still held a sense of identity for me. Having no other choice, I soon became proficient at yielding, surrendering, letting go, releasing, and relinquishing. Literally everything in my life was obliterated. Nothing was left intact.

As I languished in bed, my mantra or inner chant became "Yield to God." What else could I do? I would visualize the sunny, gold-colored yield signs on all the roads all over the country and then try to imagine how people would respond upon approaching an intersection and reading this message. As you can see, I had plenty of time for my imagination to run rampant. But the result was the development of a thriving, exotic, and whimsical inner world.

Within six months of the advent of this alien enemy, my finances were depleted; my practice, deceased; my health, ravaged. Friends, initially so supportive, began to resume their lives and only occasionally checked in. My family and friends sincerely wanted to do something to help, but the fact was that I was inconsolable. Nothing helped. I found no solace in anything that anyone said or did. The darkness was as black as an eclipse.

I was forced to live a monastic life for over two years. Surrounded by four walls, isolated from the outside world, and physically unable to do very much of anything, I could only lie prone, meditate, and pray. The only place to go was inward. The only thing I could do was think. I delved deeper and deeper into remote regions of my being. All of my attention was completely centered on God. Everything else had been stripped away, and that was all that I had left. Somehow, it just was not enough. I wallowed in self-pity and frequently jousted with despair.

Years before, while in a New York bookstore, I had been drawn to an old, colorfully illustrated book on the biblical story of Job. I had no idea why I was attracted to this book or why I bought it that day. It sat on a shelf unread for years. This was yet another example of divine guidance and syncronicity, even though at the time I was oblivious to it. After months of illness, thoughts of this book kept haunting me. I took it down from its dusty place on the bookshelf and began to read it.

It told the story of a "perfect and upright" Jewish man who lived in Judea between 500 and 400 B.C. In poetic and picturesque language, the book recounted how Satan wagered with God that Job's piety and faith could not endure extreme disaster or pain. God accepted the wager, and Job went on to suffer the loss of his wealth, wife, children, and health. He became concerned with both the causes of his own suffering and the explanation for the pathos of human life. He lamented, "Why is it that good people suffer so much affliction in life?"

Job's friends sought the reason for his suffering in Job himself, but Job searched for the reason in the nature of human life and in God. Job's friends were not willing to acknowledge that his affliction was completely unmerited. They argued that his suffering was either a punishment for a natural human imperfection in him, as in all humanity, or a disciplinary measure designed for Job by God in order to refine and deepen his nature.

Job refuted his friends, asserting that they had failed to prove that he deserved his pain. He continued to lament, "Why is it that the wicked prosper?

Why is it that dishonesty and cruelty seem to triumph in the world?" Job refused to believe his friends' arguments that he was being punished and strongly believed that there was no exact correlation between a person's conduct and his or her fate.

His deepest need was for faith, and this he achieved. Throughout the ordeal and all of his questioning and agony, he held on to precious memories of the times when he had walked in the light through the darkness of life and when God's visitation had elevated and preserved his spirit. Upon this conviction, he rebuilt his faith—a faith based upon vision rather than upon sight—and he no longer pursued the answers to the sad questions of earthly existence.

As a reward for his unwavering faith, God gave Job twice as much as he had before. He was blessed with a long life and lived happily ever after.

There were many times during my personal Armageddon that I fell to my knees and wept. I felt crucified and grieved that God had forsaken me. During this "dark night of the soul," I tenuously clung to my faith and tried to understand the meaning and purpose of this trial by fire. I reminded myself over and over about the experiences I had recently had and the advice that I had been given, "Keep the light, even in the darkness." These prophetic words and this thought were all that gave me the strength to endure.

The story of Job still rings true even after two thousand five hundred years. This is the beauty of these timeless stories that were meant to teach, inspire, and guide. We all try to make sense out of tragedy and suffering. We labor to cope with and understand adversity. Most of us reach out to some intangible higher being to safeguard ourselves or someone we love when threatened with misfortune.

Years before, I had seen devout atheists suddenly become quite religious when confronted with a terminal diagnosis. When we feel trapped, boxed in, surrounded by all sides, and looking for a way out, eventually, we must look up.

Here I was, a front-row spectator to the annihilation of the life that I had known. I asked the same questions as Job, and they raised a firestorm of uncertainty, dissent, and an unappeasable thirst for answers. His prayers were also mine. Has anything really changed?

I likened myself to a caldron of lentils cooking over a divine fire, softening, vitalizing, the pungent flavor of my essence amplified by the caustic and burning heat of the illness. Sometimes, we are refined in the furnace of affliction.

I continued the pilgrimage to the center of my being as there was no place else to go. I was incapable of doing anything but lying in bed, meditating and praying. I repeatedly mulled over the Mentor's first words, "Keep the light, even in the darkness." Now they made sense. Though I had descended into the most coal-black place I could imagine, I tried to focus on the light of my own soul and not the pain pounding my physical form.

The fact was I was still en route home. I just could not recognize it. It was to be a long and painful journey, a steep, rocky climb back up. But in the questing, I was there. My struggle and my strength arose from the same source. I was soon to learn about the gifts that can be found in suffering and that true healing is returning home.

The Gift of Suffering

> *"It has done me good to be somewhat parched by the heat and drenched by the rain of life."*
>
> —*Longfellow*

The days and nights that marked elapsing time blurred together into what seemed like one long, monotonous, and barren malaise. This unwelcome intermission in my life was not really a moratorium on living, but just one way that life may express itself. The mystique of it all is what makes it so phenomenal.

Nearly twenty-six homebound months passed before I began to see a gradual improvement in my health. The illness had taken a dramatic toll. I still looked and felt like a photograph that had been left out in the sun, faded beyond recognition. Feeling bankrupt on every level, physically, emotionally, financially, and spiritually, my coping skills had worn thin. Yet somehow, I managed to begin a slow emergence from the acrid environment of my sickbed and resume normal daily tasks despite the continued fatigue and pain.

Slow steps toward recovery began, and some life was returning to my ailing and fragile body. As the recuperation process progressed, I embarked upon another renewal. It seemed as if I were perpetually starting yet another cycle of symbolic death and rebirth. A resurrection was occurring, and like a phoenix rising from the ashes, I was spreading my broken wings and beginning to take flight. I was so incredibly grateful for the minutest things—

taking a walk, feeling the sunshine, looking at the ocean. My life had been devoid of these commonplace activities for far too long. These simple pleasures meant so much. As I began to regain some normal functioning, I found myself deeply engaged in gratitude at every moment. It was joy as never before, pure joy for the privilege of being alive and being able to participate in life's sacred offerings.

One thing we can definitely count on in life is change. Once again, the life I had known was extinct, and I was faced with rebuilding, redefining, and rehabilitating myself. This time, all of the external structures had to be rebuilt as well. Prior to becoming ill, I had viewed myself as a strong and majestic tree, always thriving in the rays of the sun, expanding and sprouting branches that reached out for more space, growing shiny, new tender leaves, shedding old ones, strengthening the bark on its body as it aged, and developing a distinctive character through years of inclement weather. The tree spontaneously blossomed and bore fruit because that was its function.

Well, over the past seven years, this tree had been whacked by a divine chainsaw and was merely a half-alive stump, struggling to grow back even stronger and more durable. The pruning had been traumatic, but I could now see new, burgeoning green shoots once again sprouting and sturdy, powerful roots reaching into the depths of the earth for nourishment.

The illness was serving as a purifier, an antiseptic that eradicated and scrubbed away obstacles inhibiting the Divine from flowing into my soul. These obstacles are those barriers existing in one's character that impede development of the spiritual self. Character cannot develop by just hoping. It requires systematic cultivation through a long-term educational process, and that process should be one that is uniquely self-defined, not dictated by others.

Our human shortcomings—self-centeredness, envy, and impatience, for example—do not allow for the highest expression of the spirit. Lack of self-control and discipline allows the lower nature (our more primitive instincts) to run amuck and pulls the spirit downward instead of up toward the light. For many people, including myself, there comes a time when our own inner, divine light may assail the body with brutal force in order to strengthen, subdue, and renew it. We suffer pain and agony as we are stripped of the habitual patterns, routines, and attachments that keep us from the full expression of our spirit and union with our Source.

Since my first walk with Universal Mind, I had been steadily peeling off layers of stagnant conditioning, layers of insulation that blocked the light from entering or radiating from within me. For better or worse, Universal Mind is primarily concerned with the evolution of our soul and uniting all of us, not necessarily with what we want or what is comfortable. In the lyrics of one of their songs, the Rolling Stones conveyed a cosmic insight, "You can't always get what you want, but you get what you need." I certainly was not pleased with my circumstances, but with complete faith in the benevolence of Universal Mind, I deeply understood that whatever happens is always for the highest good.

I began to experience a fusion and expansion that led to a growing identification with the suffering of humanity. I was not exempt from tragedy and sorrow as I had so naively thought. My role was supposed to be that of doctor, caretaker—not patient. Nevertheless, calamity had stumbled upon me, and it was most humbling.

"If you are not suffering with your brothers throughout the world
who are in the midst of strife and turmoil, you are missing
one of the greatest revealing agencies of all time."
—*The Tibetan in Alice Bailey's* Serving Humanity

Now it was my turn to ask the age-old questions "Why am I suffering?" and "Why does anyone suffer?" And the answers to those questions began to unfold, clarified, at least for me. It came to me that my illness was, in essence, a training program, with a curriculum expertly and uniquely designed for me and co-directed by my own soul and Source. The purpose of this instruction was to assist in the building of new internal structures, to erect a place inside myself where Universal Mind could comfortably reside. There is no room for the full expression of spirit if our minds and hearts are filled with the clutter of everything else. The old buildings must be dismantled and razed because they are monuments to our separated self—the self that has forgotten that it is part of the physical body of God.

When we are confronted with adversity in life, we are faced with choices. We may choose to assume the role of the victim, which allows only for helplessness, self-pity, and usually little or no growth. On the other hand, we can choose to perceive all adversity and affliction as divine guidance and a training that serves to percolate the potentiality for change and development. The ultimate goal is to bring us into closer rapport with our true selves and develop into more loving human beings.

"Once afflictions are no other than enlightenment,
one can ride on the waves of birth and death in peace.
One can travel on the boat of compassion through
the ocean of delusion with the smile of non-fear."
—*Thich Nhat Hanh*

I had definitely been brewing in a divine pot, and at times, the heat was scorching.

The trials of life, which we must all endure, can be stoically tolerated, or we can be dragged kicking and screaming all the way through. Alternatively, they can be used as grist for the mill of our spiritual selves and the evolution of our soul. The reality is that in the end no one gets through this life unscathed, so we might as well reap whatever benefits we can from the hardships.

Although suffering is grueling and makes our personalities and ego extremely unhappy, the blessings and gains for the evolution of the soul are immense. It is important to stay focused on the bigger picture. Suffering and adversity are not random and meaningless. They mysteriously exist to teach us to listen to our inner inspiration and voice. Our pains and yearnings are indwelling gifts that are meant to be used as an inner gyroscope, a tool for guidance.

Just as the nerves in our skin serve as monitors to warn us to stay away from hot or sharp objects, we possess an internal pilot that is always steering us in the right direction. This navigator is meant to orient us, map out the route, and escort us toward a life that is embroidered and embellished with the Divine.

So, the big question looming was "How do I find my own map?"

In my case, I considered the problems distressing me the most. Because of the illness, four areas were particularly difficult to cope with. They were social isolation, the inability to exercise and stay fit, being unable to work and the resulting financial difficulty, and enduring the physical pain and fatigue of the illness itself. Here was my map!

The map was encoded in the problem itself. I was to transmute these "problems" into wisdom, these dilemmas into knowledge. This was the map I had been given to follow to strengthen myself spiritually. This task was such a scholastic and arduous feat that it made my doctoral endeavors look like menial child's play.

❧❧ The Silver Lining

First, I sought to understand the benefits I could derive from social isolation. Isolation is an ancient practice in all religious traditions. Whether an Indian aesthetic sits in a cave in the Himalayas, a Catholic nun cloisters herself in a convent, a Buddhist monk is sequestered in a hilltop monastery, or Henry David Thoreau sits in the woods, all are removing themselves from the stimulation of daily life and a hectic world. This withdrawal allows the seeker to live in relative quiet, without distractions, and spend time in deep contemplation. Eliminating external distractions promotes a deep knowing of oneself and thus, one's Source. In other words, we must be alone to discover that we are not alone. We cannot reach our full potential or self-actualize without at least checkering our life with solitude.

I certainly am not advocating a solitary life. Interpersonal relationships are essential. To be excessively alone would contradict one of the primary purposes of life, learning about healthy, loving human relationships. However, due to circumstances beyond my control and forces at work beyond my comprehension, I was leading a monastic life. This is what I had been given for this moment in time. How much mileage I got out of it was my choice. I soon found that in solitude fertile ground was created for my soul to flourish. In solitude, I revealed and exposed myself as I truly AM, not how I wanted myself to be or be seen. My perpetually analytical mind was silenced. I was able to understand that true spirituality is a state of being, not a statement of achievement.

During my years of seclusion, I learned how to stand alone and be fully self-sufficient without succumbing to the impulse of conforming to the environmental influences or expectations of others. The only approval I needed was celestial. The inordinate tendency to please others at the expense of personal integrity usually stems from the fear of being alone. We sometimes say "yes" when we mean "no" because we are so afraid of social isolation.

Why are we so fearful of being quiet, turning inward, and contacting those inner depths which are so life-enhancing? When we are willing to penetrate the superficial veneer and plunge into an exploration of the inner world, only then can we access the mystical consciousness, our soul nature, our true selves, which on some level, we have always known.

"A wise man is never less alone than when he is alone."
—*Jonathan Swift*

During this time, I also learned that solitude and aloneness are not the same as loneliness. The unsettling and undesirable feeling of loneliness does not necessarily stem from being alone or a lack of contact with others. It is, first and foremost, a lack of connection to ourselves and ultimately a lack of connection to our Source. You see, the reality is that we are never really alone. Our Mentors are always with us, guiding, inspiring, and teaching. We are never alone because we are part of the family of humanity. We are never alone because we are joined with all living things. This was the gift of the isolation. At last I could see it, and more importantly, learn from it, believe in it, and live it.

The second problem I had identified as a component of my spiritual map was the inability to exercise and stay fit. This had been an extremely important goal in my life, and I had devoted part of every day to staying in tiptop condition.

Due to the illness, my muscles had withered and atrophied. I could no longer go to dance classes, jog, lift weights, scuba dive, ski, or participate in all the sports that I loved so much. Where was the gift in this? Originally, it felt only like deprivation and loss. Aside from the obvious issues of vanity, unconsciously, and on much deeper levels, I was grappling with a fear of death. As long as we are healthy, we can maintain a false notion that we can stave off that terrifying event and try to believe that death is not potentially just around the corner for all of us.

Each problem presented a different level of difficulty with respect to transmutation from a lower perspective to a higher one. This one vexed me for a long time. I had seen and heard the phrase "I am not my body, but spirit" for years in literature and in lectures, but it was an intellectual concept, a truth that I had agreed with but had had little practical value for me.

My body was not currently a very useful vehicle, or so I thought. I had to ask myself, "Useful for what?" True, it was inoperative for the activities that I just mentioned, but it was in perfect form for the lessons that I was to learn and other activities that I needed to do, like research and writing.

Although I had walked with Universal Mind and experienced soul contact, I had not yet learned to live in a way that negated the hindrances and limitations of the physical body. So instead of avoiding the issue of death, I tackled the subject directly and studied it as I had always studied anything that was mysterious, inexplicable, and intriguing. I pondered and contemplated it until I gained an elevated understanding and came to a satisfactory conclusion.

It just did not seem logical to me that a life event as universal as death, one that every living thing must experience, was so nebulous and feared. There just had to be a point to it. It had to figure into the grand scheme of the universe somehow. Through a long period of intense investigation, and with assistance from the Mentor, I began to understand that death is only a brief pause in an ongoing process of accumulating experience in the evolutionary cycles of our soul. I came to view it as an adventure as we transition from one state of consciousness to another. To put it simply, death is merely change. It is a short, yet sensational commute into a more subtle and refined form, into an unrestricted and expansive world.

The Mentor had explained to me that death is the creative process of moving forward, of shifting energy, of metamorphosing, like a caterpillar into a butterfly. But regardless of this transition, we remain ourselves, our true selves. Individuality is not lost. I was assured that when we find ourselves on the other side, or living in this parallel dimension, we reconnect with those people who have been most important to us both in the most recent life and also throughout many lives. Our relationships are imperishable and ageless. So if you divorce your spouse and think that the relationship is over, guess again.

It was also explained to me that because our physical brains no longer impede consciousness or create a false barrier of separateness, we are able to be fully aware of those still living on the physical plane. We have the ability to perceive those people and sense their thoughts and emotions at will. Somehow, that knowledge was so comforting.

I was also a bit surprised to learn that death occurs based on the insistence of our own souls. Neither our personality nor our environment is in charge of the timing of that decision; it is our soul's decision, even though our ego may protest. It is a decision based on what is most optimal for our evolution. If we perceive death from the soul's point of view, there is no such thing, just change and transition.

> *"People fail to relate death and sleep. Death, after all is*
> *only a longer interval in the life of physical plane functioning;*
> *one has only 'gone abroad' for a longer period."*
> —*Djwhal Khul*

The third problem was my inability to work and the resulting financial difficulty. Could there possibly be a silver lining to this horrendous problem? So often we define ourselves by what we do rather than who we are. We tend to amass external accomplishments to bolster sagging self-esteem rather than define ourselves by our character and spiritual development. However, the truly great men and women throughout history are revered not so much for what they did, but for what was in their heart. Ghandi, St. Francis, Buddha, and Mother Teresa are examples of saintly people whose influence continues to make a mark because of their distinguishing inner qualities, which then became visible to us through their deeds and works.

I had to incorporate into my training program a shift away from deriving my identity from my profession, away from the role of doctor, and again tread the same tapering path inward. As professed in the old saying "All roads lead to Rome," all problems in life find their solution internally. It seemed that part of my apprenticeship was geared toward helping me to understand that any path I was traveling on had to eventually lead right back to myself.

Consequently, I began to focus on my internal achievements rather than on my external exploits and accomplishments. What weakness in character did I have, and which could I conquer? Just for starters, I tackled arrogance, prejudice, and intolerance. I battled these as a knight would slay a dragon, aspiring for humility, kindness, and forgiveness to reign in their place.

Since I was not able to work, I had plenty of leisure time and many idle hours, some of which I spent constructively on formal meditation practices. Meditation brings our instincts, intellect, and intuition into creative alignment and permits us to experience a conscious union with our Source. It is a potent and effective mode of transportation into higher states of consciousness. It is primarily through meditation that we develop the sensitivity to contact our Mentors, who, most assuredly, are there. Meditation allows for profound changes in the central nervous system. It is now common knowledge that it can lower blood pressure and relieve headaches and gastrointestinal problems. It also helps to create a state of inner equilibrium and assists our minds in obtaining jurisdiction and mastery over our emotional reactions. After some time, meditation practices can aid us in developing increased control of the lower nature, that part of all of us that causes most of our troubles.

Within months of continuous and disciplined practice, I found that the effects of my meditation lasted throughout the day and I retained a sense of calm and steadiness even through stressful events. Meditation seemed to hasten, more than any other single spiritual practice, the retention of higher states of consciousness and the stabilizing of undesirable emotions.

But how was it possible that financial ruin could be a blessing in disguise? I learned how to simplify my life by extricating myself from the endless and always escalating desire for material luxuries. Ultimately, there was not very much that I really needed, just a lot of things that I wanted. I worked on transmuting the old desires for affluence into a sincere longing for the earnest expression of my soul. Material aspirations and wishes were uplifted and transformed into prayer.

Striving to shed the desire for upward mobility which is so typically American, I sought to derive pleasure from the simple beauty of nature, random acts of kindness to and from others, the joy of companionship, and gratitude for everything that I did have. As a result, my cup became half-full, not half-empty. It really is true that the best things in life are free!

The fourth major challenge presented by my illness was learning to perceive severe physical pain and debilitating fatigue as an opportunity for growth. Each problem seemed to present a higher level of difficulty to conquer, but this one was almost victorious because the pain that besieged me could not be eluded for even an hour. Physical suffering was a constant visitor and a most unwelcome one at that. But it was there, and it was there for a reason.

From the relentless torment, I learned courage. In refusing to succumb and fall victim to this illness, I developed determination, tenacity, and a staunchness of spirit. All were necessary to get through the day and not be obliterated by the pain. I was determined not just to cope well, but to heal and restore my health completely. Because of this illness, because of this suffering, I had deeply changed. Would I have accomplished such radical improvement in my character had I not been so ill? Frankly, it is doubtful. Of course, it is not necessary to suffer in order to change for the better, but it is undeniably the most influential and motivating factor for most of us.

Though many of us pray only when we are deeply troubled or seek divine guidance just when in need, I gradually became accustomed to praying ceaselessly—when I was distressed, when I was grateful, and particularly, when I was joyous. The greatest gift that I had ultimately received through all of the suffering was a more resolute and steadfast relationship with myself and my Source. I came to the profound realization that, without a doubt, there is meaning and purpose in every single event in life, and especially in those we might initially perceive as negative.

Pain is built into the system by Nature. It is a divine fire that purifies and purges those aspects of ourselves that prevent growth, progress, and the unfolding of the fragrant flower within. There is an intelligence in the universe that is beyond our comprehension that organizes, creates, and influences all of life. The whole of life is for the solitary purpose of advancing human evolution and the evolution of all living things.

Universal Mind is only concerned with the ripening and development of our soul, and sometimes the lessons are incredibly hard. In the midst of my personal adversity, I managed to unearth serenity, joy, and meaning. Ironically, all of the suffering inevitably helped to irradiate my life, lighten my burdens, and strengthen my character and link with humanity. What greater gift could there be?

The Shaman's Grail

"Don't turn your head. Keep looking at the bandaged place. That's where the light enters you. And don't believe for a moment that you're healing yourself."

—*Jelaluddin Rumi*

Six months later, my health had been upgraded from unbearable to endurable, but the illness still coiled tightly around me and squeezed with the gothic embrace of a serpent. It would not release its reptilian, wrenching grip. I had tried every known and obscure remedy to no avail. Countless trips to doctors, noxious synthetic medications, acupuncture, homeopathy, and Chinese herbal medicine all failed to yield any definitive results. Despite the strong faith I had in alternative treatments, they too proved to be vain attempts at healing myself.

Eventually, I learned to adapt to the physical limitations and adjust my life to accommodate and tolerate the symptoms. I came to a point of dispassionate acceptance and coped fairly well with my sordid predicament, but every day was still a daunting struggle.

While resting at home one day, I received a phone call from close friends living in Maui, Hawaii. They were planning on traveling abroad for six weeks and asked if I would be interested in housesitting and taking care of their pets while they were away. Despite my weakened condition, I jumped at the offer for a short sabbatical and a change in environment.

It was not long before I found myself in Maui, driving from the airport in a rented four-wheel-drive jeep up a steep, undulating mountain trail through torrents of pounding rain. Barely able to see through the streaming curtain of water, I stoically maneuvered the jeep through the muddy path that laughably was called a road. Ascending a mammoth ridge, I passed by the borders of enchanting, emerald-green rain forests carpeted with lush, prolific ferns and abutted by spiraling, jagged peaks with boulder-strewn pillars that plunged into the ocean. The wooded areas had thickets of curious native plants that I had never seen before. Occasionally, I caught a glimpse of and breathed in the sweet-scented perfume of enormous crimson and baby-blue blossoms gleefully being drenched by the downpour.

By the time I arrived at the house, the storm had diminished to a misty drizzle, and I could see the panoramic view from the driveway. The property was completely isolated, so remote that the nearest neighbor was over a mile away. I stood for a moment in the soft, warm air and tepid rain to drink in the sheer magnitude of the vista before me.

The quaint wooden house was camouflaged by the surrounding dense vegetation. A festive tangle of flowers and fruit trees wrapped around the property. Designed in a classic Japanese-style architecture, it was nestled precariously into the side of a rocky bluff. The cliff abruptly dropped down to meet the Pacific, which on that day, was churning violently and crashing against the boulders below. Nature seemed irate. It was invigorating and somewhat intimidating.

Cold and wet, I slipped the key into the door, grabbed my luggage, and promptly settled into the master bedroom, as my friends had graciously insisted. My energy depleted after flying six thousand miles and changing planes four times, I gratefully sunk into the canopied, four-poster bed.

Early the next morning, the blinding glare of the sun announced the daybreak and prodded me awake. I looked up to see lofty cathedral ceilings with exposed cedar rafters. An effusion of sunbeams fluttered in through a huge picture window much like searchlights scanning the room. The warmth of the rays, magnified by the glass, caressed my weary body.

I opened the sliding doors that led to a picturesque verandah to find, because of the altitude, that it was quite chilly. From the bedroom, I could see the patina of a glassy, aquamarine ocean which reflected and fused with a salmon-colored sky. Several small islands jutted out of the sea, resembling lonely, marooned children who had drifted away from the mother earth that had bore them. It was paradise found!

My first day there, I could not wait to explore the island. Another dear friend, David, also lived in Maui, so I set off to see him. He had learned of my medical problems and had offered to help if he could. Prior to my arrival, he had arranged for me to meet a Peruvian shaman that was briefly visiting the island. David seemed confident that meeting this person would be beneficial to my health in some way. I was not. The knowledge I had about shamans was limited to the few general facts that I had learned from an anthropology class taken during my undergraduate studies.

The rudimentary information that I remembered was that shamans, or "medicine men" as they are called in some cultures, are purported to possess certain knowledge and ancient techniques to help maintain well-being and promote healing. It is claimed that they have the ability to enter non-ordinary states of reality at will to obtain hidden knowledge, access information about future events, and improve health. These abilities and skills, as well as their accompanying rituals, are usually passed down through generations or learned through apprenticeship. These practices are as old as human consciousness itself, predating the earliest recorded civilizations by thousands of years.

Being open to meeting interesting people and desirous of doing anything or going anywhere to improve my health, I agreed to the meeting. I must confess that I expected little from the encounter. It seemed that I was again grasping at straws, but one more attempt did not seem to matter.

Anxious to see my old friend, I stood on the front porch of David's home and knocked on the lacquered, red front door. It swung open, and he greeted me with a jubilant smile and an engulfing hug. We had not seen each other in quite some time and had a lot of catching up to do.

David politely escorted me into his immaculate and beautifully furbished home. As I entered the living room, sitting piously on the couch, were four Peruvian Indians. They ranged in age from the early twenties to late forties. They spoke absolutely no English and had never before ventured outside their home in Cusco, a small city located several hours from majestic Machu Picchu, the site of the "Lost City of the Incas." With the stiff posture of alert soldiers, they nervously and uniformly stood up to welcome me. They were impeccably dressed in vividly colored traditional Peruvian attire and were all clutching primitive, handmade musical instruments. It was a definite photo opportunity, and I was, unfortunately, without my camera.

Much awkwardness followed as David and I both haltingly tried to communicate with our meager high-school-level Spanish. Wachan, the shaman of the group and translator, had not yet returned from a walk in the mountains.

The four appeared childlike, innocent, and overwhelmed by Western technology. The garbage disposal and a leaf blower were objects of much discussion, fascination, and laughter. They playfully insisted that David and I explain how everything worked and why Americans needed so many mechanical gadgets. I loved their simplicity and naiveté. It was charming.

When we sat down around a large antique oak table for lunch, I could not help but notice how flawlessly well-mannered they were. Their gracious attention to etiquette was contagious. The six of us waited with anticipation for the sumptuous vegetarian meal that David had prepared. A seventh chair, next to me, remained empty. Just as we were about to begin eating, Wachan sauntered in and unintrusively slipped into the vacant seat.

Much more sophisticated and worldly, he was a remarkable contrast to the others. His physical appearance was fiery and flamboyant. My attention was momentarily diverted by this eccentricity, though he possessed the same air of correctness and decorum as the others. Despite his overpowering looks, he stood a diminutive 5'4" with a presence that had an unaffected, carefree, and earthy quality. His facial features were unmistakably Incan, as was his leathery brown skin and tousled coarse black hair that was loosely woven into a long braid that flowed down his back. Around his neck were several strands of bizarre-looking orange and black seeds. The finishing touch was a tattered red and gold hand-woven sash that wrapped around his waist and dangled down his right leg.

We went through the usual brief introductions, and through his translations, I could now speak freely to the others. As Wachan turned his head, I noticed that lodged in his left ear lobe was a large cork. The lobe had been somehow stretched and misshapen to accommodate it. Several days later, I learned from Fladimir, the youngest of the group, that this was a sign of nobility in the Incan culture.

Lingering around the table after lunch, David and I had a lot of questions that we wanted to ask Wachan about traditional Peruvian healing techniques, but unexpectedly, the conversation quickly drifted to a discussion on dreams.

"Dreaming is not always what people think it is, and the life that we have at night is certainly not what the psychologists would like to believe," Wachan began.

I knew that this comment was meant for me. "Then what do shamans believe dreams are?" I asked.

"For centuries, dreams were the medium of prophets, who saw sacred visions in them. Many indigenous tribes believe that dreams are not an individual experience, but a collaborative event meant to be utilized by the whole community. They contain precious information that may be used as guidance for the group in matters of daily life or even survival. The villagers perceive themselves as a single, multifaceted unit, and each person's dream is just a splinter of the dreaming mind of the community. Each dream contributes to the weaving of the fabric of that society," he explained as we drank Hawaiian coffee.

Wachan became increasing animated as he continued, "There are many types of dream states, but four are the most important. The first kind usually occurs during the first two and the last two hours of sleep. These dreams are just remnants of the day's thoughts and memories. Worries, concerns, and frustrations continue to be active in the brain at night. These dreams are an attempt to resolve inner conflicts, desires, or unresolved emotions that are left over from the day."

Unimpressed, I responded, "That sounds very psychological."

"Right. That is the first part," he said with much self-assurance. "The second type of dreams are those that are true memories. They penetrate into the ancient past and are recollections of previous lives. It is difficult for us to remember prior lives in our conscious, waking state, but when we are asleep, we have access to the embryonic memories of the spirit and can recall past experiences exactly as they happened. These dreams can be very enlightening."

Now he was starting to get my attention. "What is the third kind?" I asked, thinking that the conversation was getting more metaphysical every minute.

Looking at me very intensely, he replied, "The third kind are those dreams that tap into the plethoric, collective consciousness. They are telepathic dreams. We may wake up in the morning remembering real communication with others or actual events that other people have experienced and then attribute these memories to ourselves. We can pick up the random thoughts of other people or groups of people because thoughts are actually physical phenomena. There are many anecdotal stories of people who know each other and have the same dream on the same night. This is possible because their consciousness is literally wandering around in the same place. Of course, you know that there is really only One Mind, so at night our consciousness is free of the encumbrance of our personalities and has the liberty to roam and be linked with all of humanity. We are all, in fact, inseparable, and during sleep, we are able to fully experience this."

David chimed in, "And the fourth?"

"The fourth kind is the most important," Wachan mused. "It is the time when the soul, or etheric body, actually liberates itself. This immaterial body separates from the physical body and travels in another dimension. The dreamer is able to do very normal things in this plane of existence. He or she might seek out someone that is missed or find someone to harm, if so inclined. Mental work that is initiated during the day is continued at night. What happens is based largely upon the wishes and desires of the person. If the yearnings are of a high-minded, virtuous nature, the dreamer will travel to incredible spiritual realms. If not, the yearnings will bring the dreamer to places just to try to satisfy longings. This happens almost every night to everyone and explains how blind people, even those blind from birth, can have vivid visual dreams."

"Sometimes the etheric body snaps back into place too quickly and feels almost like a thud when it returns," he explained. "The rapid reentry might cause a mild jolt. Perhaps you have experienced that. We are actually very active at night—visiting places and interacting with people living in the physical world as well as those who are not. When we are sleeping, sometimes we can make contact with our Teachers, those elevated beings that help and guide us."

"The highest form of dreaming occurs when the person's consciousness and etheric body actually enter into the primordial, divine realms and retrieve information while traipsing through. This knowledge and wisdom seep into the mind during these nocturnal visits and are remembered in the form of a dream. Many mystics and shamans go to these places at will during the night and lucidly recover profound truths and revelations. These kinds of dreams explain how people can know things about places they have never been to," Wachan explained.

I had so many questions. "What are nightmares? Are they purely psychological?"

"Not exactly. Nightmares usually occur when the spirit is not able to influence its nature, aspirations, and goals upon the personality. They are caused by a conflict between the higher and lower self. A duel is being fought in the deep recesses of the psyche, but please understand that the real war is between the soul and the personality. So, basically, a dream is a reply to an inquiry that our true being has not yet learned to consciously ask."

During the whole conversation, Fladimir was stretched out on the couch, looking a bit bored because we were speaking in English and he did not understand a word. He interrupted, "Tonight is the night of the June full moon. It is a time of great cosmic power, and we are planning a very sacred ceremony up in the mountains. Would you like to join us?"

I was a long way from having my curiosity satiated about Wachan's beliefs about the nature of dreams, but was excited by the invitation. It seemed time to change the subject, so we did.

As we started to plan the trip, I could only marvel at Wachan's metaphysical philosophies and his ability to articulate complex ideas in a simple way. Looking forward to spending more time with all of them, I had a feeling that this evening had the potential to turn into a very exciting adventure.

The location that they had chosen for the ritual was not accessible by car so David had arranged to borrow horses from a neighboring farm. He had reserved one for me, too, accurately anticipating that I would go. Although we all had a great deal of riding experience, the owner of the stable insisted on giving us brief instructions. "Keep the reins in your hands at all times. Keep your feet in the stirrups, and your mind in the middle." Little did he realize that the guidance he was giving was not just about horses.

Before the light of day acquiesced to the twilight, we were collecting our gear, mounting seven very aristocratic looking horses and beginning a caravan further up the steep, treacherous mountain. As the sure-footed horses steadily triumphed over the rocky ground, I began to develop a very congenial relationship with Shahzadi, the chestnut-colored mare that I was riding. I remembered that during my walk with Universal Mind I had realized that all animals are fully conscious, intelligent, and sentient beings, and I wanted very much to be respectful of this beautiful and noble creature of God.

It is a well-known fact that mammals experience anger, jealousy, grief, and happiness. Research now suggests that parrots, chimpanzees, and dolphins are capable of mastering complex intellectual concepts including rudimentary language skills. Parrots have been known to name up to fifty objects, recognize colors and numbers, and understand the concept of same and different. Dogs are able to sense when a person is about to have an epileptic seizure and communicate a warning. In fact, a large canine training program has been established just for this purpose.

We are able to slaughter animals and use them for experimentation only because we perceive them as "dumb" and unable to understand the environment around them. This could not be further from the truth.

I wanted to make sure that Shahzadi felt comfortable carrying me on her back, so we engaged in long talks as we clambered up the embankment.

She seemed to understand when I explained that I was ill and needed her help. A natural bond and affinity developed between us.

We rode for several hours and darkness was setting in. The milky light from the full moon gave us just enough illumination to make our way to our destination, a pristine, primeval-looking plateau almost at the summit and just on the edge of an ancient volcanic crater. The peak of the dormant volcano soared so high above sea level that gauzy, vaporous alabaster clouds lazily floated by. The stillness and obscurity of the clearing was enlivened by the cryptic shrill of a large bluish-gray bird. Its shrieks seemed doleful and forlorn.

The location that they had picked looked almost otherworldly and somewhat like my imagined version of Shangri-La, the magical and mythical lost land of utopian beauty. The terrain was composed of slate-colored volcanic soil that had propagated rich vegetation over the centuries. The raw majesty of the landscape left me breathless. I was physically weak and saddle sore from the grueling ride, but the scenery was so impressive and soul stirring that I was able to ignore my discomfort. We tied up the horses and began to unload the gear we had brought with us.

Exhausted, I took out a hand-woven straw mat from the supply bag and sat down on the cool ground. The temperature was rapidly dropping as the sun had already set. After locating a blanket, I wrapped it around me to fend off the cold air and then scanned the area to become more familiar with my surroundings. The clearing that was now our encampment was almost completely lit up by the incandescent light of the full moon, our heavenly chandelier. The lunar glow reflected off the mica embedded in the surrounding rocks. Each boulder twinkled with life and flickered in unison with the glinting stars overhead. The result was a fantastic display of a symbiotic collaboration between heaven and earth.

A small waterfall cascaded nearby. In the continuous soft murmur of the water splashing into an icy pool, I heard a rhythmical concerto which lulled me into a calm trance. I began to feel the same expansive state of mind starting again. I was never exactly sure what would prompt these states, but being close to nature usually helped. My normal perceptions again began to transform, my usual way of seeing dissolved, and the visionary realms were once more accessible.

I glanced at this ancient fountain and saw tiny prisms of light leaping from the junction where the downpour met the still water. Each one contained the full spectrum of marbled colors and had a psychedelic effect as the water swirled into little miniature whirlpools. The tiny, translucent liquid vortexes were like the black holes in space, sucking everything into themselves. Everything was animate and alive. Everything around me had an individual identity and, simultaneously, a kinship to all other things. The whole area was alive, pulsating, and throbbing with energy. I could see it in the air and feel it in the ground beneath me.

Wachan had brought several knapsacks with all kinds of implements and provisions for the ceremony. It took almost two hours for him to adorn the immediate area with the essential artifacts, and he did it with great dexterity and artistry. Tied onto the tree we were sitting under were red and blue Macaw feathers. Strategically placed on the ground were a large queen conch shell with a hole drilled into the cone and a small wooden flute. Local flowers adorned the entire site.

He started a fire with dried wood shavings from Peruvian mahogany trees and palm leaves that had been gathered at the base of the mountain. He then encircled it with small stones found nearby. All around the sitting area were clay saucers filled with various herbs and incense. Among the peculiar and intriguing mixtures were dried llama fetus, coca leaves, assorted seeds, chamomile, and sage.

When Wachan finished and everything was in place, we sat in a semicircle around the fire. Surging, pyrotechnic blue and reddish-orange flares of heat sent golden embers of light gracefully hovering above the flames. As the wood was consumed, the smoldering coals bestowed much appreciated warmth.

The Peruvians had brought all of their musical instruments with them—flutes, maracas, rattles tied in layers around their ankles, and skin drums of various sizes. They had masterfully handcrafted all of the instruments. They were primitive but very beautiful.

All seated around the fire, they began to play a sweet-sounding but rather melancholy tune, a melodious sonata that had been composed in a most unusual way. Raul had told me that the five men had traveled to the ruins of remote and ancient vine-covered Incan temples in Peru. There, they spent days in prayer and meditation until the ancestral tribal music, thousands of years old, would come to them. Past centuries would come alive as they heard and absorbed these chimerical musical tributes to the gods. They subsequently brought them back home to play only during very sacred ceremonies.

The blending, harmonizing vibrations of the instruments created an ebullient response inside of me. It felt like drinking an elixir of soothing tones. The sounds converged into a homogenized whole and began to appear visually before me. The music created waves of oscillating, rainbowy color that seemed to release energy in the atoms around us. Simultaneously, the colors in the environment were so vibrant that I could literally hear them. Miraculously, I was seeing sound and hearing colors!

In India, they have an ancient system of psychical teaching which is a form of Yoga. Learned students and teachers say that by pronouncing a certain mystical word correctly and repeatedly, one can create a vibration that has a purifying effect on the body and mind. It is believed that this one word, spoken with great and pure intent can open the gateway to the heavens. The fact that certain sounds can heal and affect our spiritual nature is an age-old premise.

Wachan sang and chanted ancient Peruvian invocations for over an hour. The breeze blew the pungent smoke from the incense in my direction and stung my eyes. I was forced to close them. The music then rushed inside of me. I was not simply hearing the vocals and musical notes. The sounds were reverberating within me and producing a vibratory resonance that was somehow affecting my physiology. The music was not emanating solely from the instruments themselves, but also from the inner depths of the men playing them.

I mentally flashed back to a vague memory of my childhood when, rare as it was, I was in temple for the High Holy Days. In Judaism, the mystical wailing call of the shofar, the blowing of a ram's horn, is intended to awaken the soul and help prayers ascend to heaven. This familiar braying sound seemed to be mingled with the other instruments. When I opened my eyes and looked up, Heber was, in fact, blowing a ram's horn, though a Peruvian version.

Wachan continued to chant and pray in his native Quechua, and despite the fact that I did not understand the language, somehow I knew the intention was to reestablish, for those moments, a cohesive unity for all of us, with ourselves and with everything around us. This must be the definition of true utopia: no separation from anything.

As the music amplified and intensified, Wachan was obviously entering into an altered state. He seemed to be opening a passageway to his heart and mind through his sung prayer. The incantations were increasingly more passionate and reaching a feverish, almost hyperbolic pitch. I opened my eyes again because I felt more heat against my face and assumed that the fire was encroaching. I could feel the temperature increasing on my left side. Instead, what I saw was Wachan, drenched in perspiration, looking very flushed, and continuing to chant as if his life depended on it. He was ablaze with emotion. The heat that I felt was emanating from his body as if he were as inflamed as the fire. I could not believe it! I quickly scanned to make sure that the source of the heat was not coming from the flames. It was not; in fact, the flames were not even close to me!

As the prayers reached their zenith, poignant tears dripped down his face, and he continued to sway in an almost orgasmic embrace with the Divine. Then the music suddenly stopped and Wachan fluidly shifted from his native tongue to English. He reached into one of the small leather pouches and retrieved three coca leaves for each of us, explaining that they represented the upper, middle, and lower spirit worlds. We were then instructed to hold them gingerly between our fingers. Earnestly, and with as much potency as we could, we were encouraged to infuse the leaves with our heartfelt prayers. We silently prayed for some time.

I could think of many things to pray for, both for myself and others, but I thought, just one would be right. There was something that I wanted very much for myself. "Yes," I thought. "I will ask for that…. Commander-in-chief, CEO of the universe, please restore my health." I knew that Universal Mind had a sense of humor and although I was being playful, this plea was completely sincere and reverent at that moment.

That was my prayer, "Please restore my health." Wachan ceremoniously took each coca leaf and one by one, placed them in a white linen cloth which represented spiritual purity. He then wrapped them up, along with the ashes from the incense and herbs, and tied them into a bundle with string. Again, he began to chant and pray, rocking back and forth and holding this parcel tenderly cupped in his hands. In that package with the ashes and leaves were the essence of our wishes, hopes, and dreams.

With much grandeur, he lit a candle, raised the bundle up in the air, and called for the spirits to hear our devout prayers and pleas for help. When he was finished, his mood lightened, as if the weight of the world had just been lifted off his shoulders. With much exuberance, he tossed the precious parcel into the fire. As the cloth burned, a cloud of smoke wafted up into the air and carried with it the ashes of the smoldering leaves tainted with our earnest petitions and praise. David and I watched with awe as the gray smoke was lifted up into the cosmos and scattered by the wind.

Unexpectedly, Wachan leaped up from the place where he had been sitting for hours, and with great abandon, he began to dance. The musicians started to play again as if on cue, and we all spontaneously found ourselves up on our feet and joining in. We laughed, twirled, and rollicked in a wild celebration of life. I felt buoyant, happier, and freer than I had been in years. We were all like joyous children—playful and undeniably euphoric. I pirouetted, gyrated, and spun like a whorling dervish. Dancing was totally effortless and uninhibited. I had enormous energy and lightness in my body and much finer motor control than usual. I threw off my shoes so I could feel the ground beneath my feet and continued to prance and leap to the zealous music. I did not feel the cold at all.

Then I remembered, "Wait a minute! I'M SICK. How is this possible?" I had not danced for seven years, yet here I was, jumping around and having a grand old time.

I turned to David with a stunned expression and cried, "I'm well!"

With a shrewd grin, he looked lovingly at me and said, "Great!"

With the arrival of dawn's first light, I felt as if I had woken up from an eerie dream. The pain and crippling fatigue in my body were gone. Incredibly, I had completely forgotten what it felt like to just be healthy.

We loaded our gear, again mounted the horses, and began the spiraling descent down the steep incline strewn with broken and shifting rocks. It seemed all too often that I metaphorically and literally climbed to great heights just to find myself back at the bottom. Such is the cyclic rhythm of life, the ebbing and flowing of the creative processes that contribute to our inevitable evolution.

As we descended, the slate-gray color of the lava rock gave way to constantly changing stratas of earth until we were riding over chalky limestone. It was now twenty degrees warmer.

We rode until we reached a secluded, crescent-shaped lagoon. The cove was isolated by soaring cliffs that thankfully shielded us from the rest of the world. The pristine beach was tinged with the Polynesian mystique of jet-black sand and was littered with smooth, bleached driftwood that created a stately design of elegant and lithe abstract sculptures. The wood was deeply embedded in this ebony shoal, but the crests rose up to form an array of twisted, luxuriant, liquid poses. They looked very much like tawny icons, carvings crafted by the master artisan, Universal Mind. From the top of the ridge flowed a wall of diaphanous fresh water that tumbled toward a rendezvous with the foaming salty sea. The two commingled in an enamel-blue, roiling ocean.

Jubilant from the evening's events and elated by the exhilarating feeling of wellness, I slid off my horse and made a mad dash to the waterfall and jumped in fully clothed. With a primal scream, David immediately followed along with the rest of the crew who jumped into the water sans clothing. Being rather modest and the only woman, I covertly disrobed under the water. Hidden from view, I threw my jeans and T-shirt upon the shore. I felt an innocent sense of purity and simplicity swimming in the crystal-clear water, a sort of elemental baptism.

Feeling very emotional, I instinctively swam off to be alone. The beloved ocean felt like home. I slipped through the water, a zephyr-like mermaid, gliding and then diving beneath the swelling waves. As I gently floated in an undulating sea, it felt as if I were enveloped in a nurturing aquatic womb. I pondered the fact that I was now well and began to understand the intrinsic process of my own illness and healing.

Illness can occur for so many reasons, environmental, genetic, infectious, or karmic, but one thing I am now sure of is that we do not "cause" our own sickness by having wrong thoughts or being a sinful person. This should be apparent when we recognize that disease exists in all of nature. Even some of our greatest saints suffered from horrible afflictions. Certainly, they did nothing to deserve ill health.

For example, in contemporary times, if an illness is caused strictly by an environmental poisoning, the illness needs to be viewed from a more global perspective. It is not that person alone who is suffering. That tiny cell in the body of God is serving as a warning to all of us that we are jeopardizing the health of humanity. That person is functioning as a human "canary in the mine," an advance intelligence system to alert all of us to danger. Unfortunately, humanity does not listen very well.

We must begin to acknowledge that there are mysterious forces at work all around and within us, streaming from the divine creative center and governing much of what happens in our lives. All things—minerals, plants, animals and humanity—are undergoing an unfathomable process of evolution through a succession of expansions. We know that the universe itself is expanding, but we typically do not think in terms of our own individual, burgeoning consciousness. It is a misconception that the evolutionary process is primarily a physical one. It is not. The true progress and unfoldment occurs on the spiritual and metaphysical plane of existence. Each and every one of us is constantly undergoing this flowering of the soul, although we are not always directly aware of it, the end result being complete and utter unity, an at-one-ment with everything and everyone.

Just as the soul is a flawless, ethereal duplicate of the body, alongside the physical world there is a complex etheric world that is its exact but non-material replica. Both are composed of physical matter. The only difference is that the etheric world, a maelstrom of energy, is constructed of a much finer and subtler substance. Humanity is metaphorically a lump of coal that is impacted, altered, and influenced by potent, guiding, and vital energies through eons of time. The ultimate goal of this evolutionary process is to emerge a diamond, symbolic of the attainment of full consciousness on the humanitarian and planetary levels.

In my case, I have come to believe that a collision of forces occurred that resulted in illness. On the one hand, great awakening energies were flooding into my soul: On the other hand, my personality, the denser aspect of the two parts, resisted the whole process. The dissension and the lack of unity and rapport between the two parts of myself resulted in a divided and disjointed state. This kind of fragmentation can produce all kinds of disease processes, which are, in fact, only a bodily method of refocusing energy.

The trials and tribulations of illness are only important insofar as they contribute to the enhancement and advancement of the soul experience. That part is up to us in terms of how we choose to interpret and handle the challenge of being ill. I have also realized that my continued animosity toward my illness only served to intensify and fuel it because energy always follows thought.

Our thoughts are actually real and tangible energy. As such, they have a definite influence upon us and the environment. When you enter a synagogue or a church, you know that it is a place that is prayed in because you can feel an atmosphere of sanctity about it. If you are attentive, you can also tell when you have entered a happy home. There is a faint impression, a sense that can be perceived and intuitively felt. By the same token, if there has been continual fighting in the environment, the hostility can be detected as well.

There are no boundaries, limits, or time constraints for our thoughts. It would take one hundred years for a beam of light to reach us from the nearest star but because the whole universe is an exalted Mind, and our individual mind is a minute particle of it, a simple thought would reach that same star instantaneously. The lack of understanding of the underlying metaphysical aspects of disease combined with emotional and psychological resistance to forward movement largely delayed my healing. True healing can potentially occur when the life force circulates without restriction, unblocking obstructions in the flow of energy and vitalizing the body. This is the basic principle of acupuncture, a Chinese medical treatment two thousand years old.

This process is also the definition of spontaneous healing which is so well documented but not clearly understood in the medical literature. Spontaneous healing is simply the body's innate and intrinsic ability to maintain and heal itself. Of course, how that exactly occurs still remains a mystery.

It is important to understand that we cannot always know the source or reason for illness, that not all disease is curable, and as unfair as it may seem, that not everyone is meant to heal in any given lifetime. We cannot know the exact meaning and purpose behind all suffering or the reason for all tragedy. We just need to have faith in the existence of a higher, impelling force that is much wiser than ourselves and completely benevolent in terms of our spiritual development.

Somehow, through sacred sounds, devotional and heartfelt prayers, and the maintenance of the true image of our Source held deep within the inner sanctum of the group, I had been healed. It is still beyond my grasp to digest the whole of this experience. I just know that it happened, and I am well. I pray that it continues.

Floating weightlessly, time seemed suspended. I gazed up at the dome of deep blue sky and breathed a joyful sigh. On the horizon hung an arc of technicolored hues. A rainbow had suddenly appeared, with one end originating in the clouds and the other alighting upon the mountaintop from which we had just descended. This was yet another sign and symbol imploring me to remember that the bridge between heaven and earth is the colorful link between our souls and our Source.

I had found my pot of gold on that mountaintop at the rainbow's end. The greatest riches were now mine, the treasure of health.

IV. Sojourns to Grace

The Divinely Abnormal

> *"God sleeps in a stone, dreams in a flower, moves in an animal and wakes in man."*
>
> —*Irenaeus*

With a renewed vigor and the remembrance of that life-altering night in Maui intricately etched into the lacework of my psyche and soul, I knew that the seemingly impossible was possible and that the inconceivable was within reach.

The restoration of my health rekindled the desire to resume the research I had begun before I had fallen ill. A compelling need to investigate and examine the ancient, universal, and mystifying phenomenon of higher states of consciousness resulted in the resuscitation of the initial draft of my studies. I had already accumulated a medley of diverse information and interviews of personal accounts, but now, I was determined to integrate all of this data and knowledge into a framework that would help mental health professionals understand that there is a colossal psychical gorge between madness and mysticism.

I wanted very much to shatter the existing obsolete and archaic belief systems that debunk the reality of mystical states, to provide what is needed to rectify the deficiencies that presently exist, and to validate and acknowledge so many people all over the world whom I affectionately refer to as the "divinely abnormal." Perhaps verification and documentation of these expanded states of awareness will help others in the future to avoid the unnecessary pitfalls of alarm, distress, and confusion.

During the seek-and-find mission for the divinely abnormal that I had set in motion, a man named Barry contacted me from Houston, Texas. Now retired, he had worked for NASA as an engineer in the aerospace industry and described an experience that came "out of the blue." After several lengthy and collaborative conversations, we became kindred spirits, allied by our deep devotion to our Source and to helping others find faith and hope.

Out of all of the beautiful and diverse experiences that I had heard, I felt that his story was one of the most classic and transformational. The following is an excerpt from one of his manuscripts:

Toto, We're Not in Kansas Anymore

For most of my life, I was immersed solely in the scientific, logical, technical mind-set. I knew nothing about personal or spiritual transformation, or growth and enlightenment, or perennial wisdom. So, although the following tale of how I encountered transformation may seem wild and fanciful, it might be helpful to someone who is attempting to understand a similar experience.

One evening, I had a very deep sensation. Something within me spoke of my needing courage and needing to submit, to give in. I tried to give in. Then, it seemed as though at my lower right, there was a door, the top half of which was either open or glass. Through this door I somehow felt I could see the whole thing, the universe, the cosmos. This was very strange. Yet I wanted very badly to see and understand. It seemed as though it was all right there, but I could not fathom it. It was blurred, out of focus.

Then I seemed to drop into a hyper-state of some sort that was smooth, fluid, deep, excited. I was enveloped in a flame.

I had a feeling of flying over other worlds, other planets, accelerating through the cosmos. Wave after wave of ecstasy came. Then, it gradually subsided. I was weak-kneed and somewhat stunned, but very quiet and calm. It seemed as if the whole cosmos surrounded and encircled me, but I could not reach it. I did not know what was going on. But what a feeling!

I had a sense that I did not reach it because I was afraid. I also somehow felt that maybe I wasn't ready. It seemed that I lacked something. I could only describe that "something" as perhaps a sort of moral maturity. I seemed to sense that I was a bit too scattered a person and that I needed to achieve a greater level of integrity.

And yet, somehow, I felt I had been close to seeing something, close to another, higher state of consciousness. And, even though it seemed more maturity was needed, there was also a sense that this higher state of consciousness had a child-like and kind of easy-going quality and a certain pleasant naiveté about it. This is in sharp contrast to the ponderous seriousness usually associated with such things. The experience itself seemed to have a positive moral and maturing effect on me; it engendered a general kindness and deeply felt OKness, a state of being which seemed to be a source of moral goodness.

All along I had this hovering cloud of skepticism. Was any of this real, or was it simply delusion? I became very tired and sunk into a deep, calm state. Then, I went into a virtually instant state of rapture, enveloped in rose-colored light. In this state, it was obvious to me that everything was both absolute and relative at once. This state went on for over an hour. Had I wanted to, I do not know that I would have even known how to get out of it. Finally, it subsided. This happened two or three more times in the next few days. Again, both absolute and relative states of being were clearly present at once. Also, I had glimpses of light, like a camera shutter very, very briefly opening and quickly shutting.

As the days went by, I would think to myself, "Submit ... submit to God," though I was not sure what that meant exactly. I started to get general feelings of being told something about the cosmos, but I could not grasp the "messages." Finally, almost in exasperation, I asked for the message, and I mentally saw this simple yellow flower near the edge of a field and heard a distinct voice. The voice or voices started telling me things. Remarkably, I found I could ask questions and get answers. Whoever was giving me the answers was a "we." It, they, whatever, kept saying "We..." Those inner voices were doing a comparable simplifying, linearizing translation, an interpretation of profound cosmic concepts, and they did it with enormous kindness, gentleness, compassion and consideration. I have never encountered anything like this quality of deep, boundless compassion and caring on the human level of existence.

As you can see, this was all becoming weirder and weirder. And yet, I was incredibly curious about this apparent state of consciousness. So, in my best adventurous determination, I pressed on. Although, once again, there was this hovering cloud of skepticism, coupled with the fact that I really did not know what I was doing. Probably, all I had going for me was a certain honest sincerity, a deep, genuine desire to KNOW.

I went through a period in which I was weeping ... weeping and muttering, "It's all true. It's all true!" over and over again. By this I meant the extended view of reality I had started to investigate. There WERE other, higher states of consciousness and other ways of perceiving reality. There was a deeper, underlying Reality to the universe, the cosmos. I now simply knew it was true, and knew it in a way I could not have otherwise imagined. It was a deep experiential "knowing," an undeniable certitude impossible to describe.

We have an inner or higher Self that is immortal and a lower self that dies, but an essence or aspect of personality remains. The purpose of our ordinary three-dimensional universe and of human life is experiential, a way to experience certain things. However, the specific details of what happens here on earth, the specific details of our lives, do not seem significant in an absolute sense to the higher entities, the "we" speaking to me. The feeling I had was that this "we" was like a community of "souls" that was sort of just sitting back and watching and experiencing certain things through us. No matter what happened, no matter how much suffering was endured, no matter how confused or bleak things could seem, in the end, everyone was absolutely safe anyway.

I asked the question, "Why is there a universe at all?" I was "told" there were endless sets of creations going on and on, round and round. There was not just one web of creation, but repeated sets of them. I slid deeper into myself. "Why is there a universe?" I got back the booming remark, "God is a Mind." Then, unbelievably, I felt myself in that mind. In that place, there was no time, no space. Everything, all reality, was in the Mind, yet it was spaceless! There were unfathomable intermeshing webs of activity. Everything was interrelated in it. I need to note that the word "mind" is just a conceptual, verbal interpretation. What was there was a far, far grander thing than the term usually connotes. Our minds are less than a shadow of it. It possesses attributes and capabilities far beyond those our ordinary consciousness can assimilate or grasp. It was an incredible gift and privilege to have seen this.

As a result of this chain of events, I came face-to-face with a huge gap between the broader view of reality presented to me and what I saw going on everywhere around me. Everyone was living with limited views of things—in a dull, flat, almost comatose world, robotically entangled in endless rounds of activities, including many designed to produce a kind of false excitement that covers up the dull flatness.

In my day-to-day work in an aerospace engineering organization, I saw much more clearly that because of people's limited views of reality, including themselves, they became mired in self-centered political motives, addicted to status and control, driven by money and issues of worthiness, etc. They have accomplished many things, but because they were mired in such petty, limited concerns, they also created endless unnecessary conflicts and problems, stayed frustrated, launched misguided activities, worked inefficiently, and lacked vision.

And, in general, I saw more clearly how this was true everywhere. Because we are stuck in limited, petty views of ourselves, others, and the world, we do not live effectively. We unknowingly create unnecessary difficulties everywhere, on all levels—in our families, our neighborhoods, companies, nations, and the entire world.

On the other hand, it seemed quite clear that if we could live with the kind of broader, more complete view I had experienced, we would be more likely to avoid many of our conflicts, problems, and frustrations. At least, they would be less severe, or we could better resolve them. We could reach higher, more interesting, more vital, more enjoyable, nobler, more satisfying states. In fact, I noticed that the few people who had anything approaching this kind of broader view (whether or not they were fully aware of it as such) tended to *live and work more effectively, in the best interest of a whole enterprise, not just themselves. They more quickly saw into the true heart of matters and took honest, effective action. I realized that there was a virtually hidden, unknown world. And I realized that you just had to see it to See it.*

Evidently, behind the everyday, mundane reality, what is going on in the universe is actually an awesome, timeless, spaceless process. This is then translated into and reflected by our ordinary world in a simplifying, almost trivializing framework by which we can then see, experience, and understand things to some degree.

I have since come to know that my experiences and insights were only minor blips relative to what is ultimately possible for any of us humans. I have also come to humbly realize that the act of having such insights can still be a long way from actually putting their implications into effect in daily life.

However, despite all our churches, synagogues, mosques, philosophies, and mythologies, hardly anyone I came into daily contact with saw any of this, and I realized what a great cultural resistance there was to it. I realized that despite Western society's many achievements, some of the very beliefs and characteristics it fosters and values not only promote unnecessary conflicts and problems but also inhibit our seeking the broader view, which is the way out of our problems.

We rely too much on Western science as the sole arbitrator of truth. Our beliefs glorify narrow, self-centered pursuits and motives and focus excessively on money and possessions. As long as we look to these beliefs and values to guide our lives and define our worthiness, we obscure the broader view and stay mired in limitation. So, to genuinely seek a broader view, something has to jar us; we somehow need to realize that we are mired in limitation, that something is deficient, amiss enough such that we deeply question and examine our beliefs and worldviews, as well as what is driving and motivating us.

Furthermore, from my own experiences, I found that even if we seek and actually manage to glimpse a broader view, we still need to continually, even more deeply, examine the beliefs, motives and worldviews that lie behind our most mundane daily thoughts and behavior. Otherwise, as the saints tell us, because initial glimpses into broader, underlying realities tend to be short and temporary, we easily remain in, or sink back into, our old ways. Unless we make a real, continual effort to uproot the old and help the new take hold, our old beliefs, habits, and motives still tend to dominate our daily thoughts and actions.

Daily, I am humbly reminded of this by my thoughts and actions. In short, I have found that despite spontaneous, glorious, transcendent visions, real, permanent transformation requires continually cleaning off muck in ordinary life.

We are each our own windows to everything we see in the universe and the reflection of the universe we see.

Mine is an old, old story, an enduring story retold endlessly in endless ways by religious founders, saints, sages, prophets, shamans, poets, and philosophers from ancient times to the present, by every culture, in every land.

This is an edited version of an elaborate and in-depth communiqué that Barry initially mailed to me. I was deeply moved and touched by his story and struck by the uncanny resemblance to my own experience and responses to it. But I want to emphasize that his personal story and others that are similar should not be looked upon as being exceptional or supernatural in any way but rather as a normal incident and result of natural spiritual evolution and growth.

Prior to this event, Barry had been aware of claims made about other states of consciousness and other forms of reality besides the ordinary one, but, being a scientist, he had remained skeptical. What makes Barry's story so credible and plausible is the consistent self-questioning that takes place throughout the ordeal. He reacts with awe and humility when faced with Universal Mind and entertains a healthy introspection and inquiry as to whether the perceptions are real or imagined. People who are delusional and psychotic do not usually question or doubt their false impressions.

More importantly, beyond the phenomena, elation, and exhilaration that may accompany these states are the transformation, awakening, and understanding that germinate from such an encounter. Barry and I remain friends and he tells me that he is still on his odyssey, for this life and for all time.

A thorough explanation of the complicated clinical distinctions between actual psychopathological states and authentic mystical events exceeds the scope of this book. However, I do want to describe the basic elements and essence of the mystical experience.

My research and review of accounts of reported mystical experiences, both ancient and contemporary, has revealed that a number of commonalties unite most authentic experiences. The following are prevailing and recurrent themes and repercussions:

1. A distinct awareness of an intelligence that exceeds and transcends all existing belief systems is recognized;

2. The experience is unexpected and temporary; it cannot be forced;

3. The external world is suddenly perceived differently than before, not as separate, but unified; a perception of congruity and universality prevails;

4. The experience produces a feeling of renewal and rebirth with an increased sense of meaning and purpose;

5. A strong conviction and faith in a higher power remains after the experience; contact with Universal Mind makes it very clear where we stand in the cosmos;

6. A certainty and confidence in immortality is instilled (upon glimpsing higher realms, we understand that consciousness does not die and that only the physical body itself is temporary); and

7. An extraordinary and unlimited expansion of intellect and an influx of knowledge ensue.

Though so many mysterious paranormal occurrences such as clairvoyant or psychic phenomena are very real, they are quite different from the experiences described above.

In the midst of the pursuit for information and anecdotes of mystical experiences, I came across a legendary and classic example of the divinely abnormal, St. Joan of Arc. Her life story exemplifies the trials, tribulations, and stigma that usually plague people who have experienced higher states of consciousness.

History has meticulously recorded the epic tale of Joan, a fifteenth-century illiterate peasant girl who, at the age of fourteen, began to hear voices and have visions. They innocently began in the summertime in her father's garden. At first, she was quite afraid, but by the third episode, she became convinced that it was the voice of a protective angel sent to help and guide her. She was hesitant to tell anyone, including the parish priest.

Joan left a detailed and precise account of her experiences, stating that the voices originated on her right side and were accompanied by a bright light. The voice repeatedly told her to help the French king, and by the age of seventeen, and not even knowing how to ride a horse, she was in command of the French army. At age nineteen, she was captured and put on trial for heresy.

Throughout the trial, Joan was assailed and castigated for claiming to hear "voices." Declaring a complete faith in God, she refused to recount anything she held as sacred and true. Tragically, she was declared a heretic and burned alive at the stake with God's name on her lips as she died. In 1920, she was canonized as a saint.

On a lighter note, one of my favorite childhood books, Dr. Seuss' *Horton Hears a Who*, illustrates, through story-telling, the potential turmoil and hardships that may arise for the divinely abnormal. Perhaps, even as a child, I sensed that this story would apply to me in some magical way in my future. It is the story of Horton the elephant, who, while happily living in the jungle, suddenly begins to hear a faint voice. He looks toward the sound but sees nothing. But then he hears it again—just a tiny cry for help. Horton looks and looks but can see only a small speck of dust blowing past him through the air. He lifts the dust speck with his trunk and places it on a very soft clover. All the other animals in the jungle start to gather around him. They laugh and make fun of him, but he is convinced that he has heard this tiny voice. Horton begins to converse with the voice and discovers that there is an entire city called Whoville living on this dust speck and that he is speaking with the mayor of the town.

The monkeys and the kangaroos call him a fool and continue to torment him. Soon, a black-hearted eagle swoops down, steals the dust speck and flies off with it in his beak. Horton chases the bird over rough mountains and begs him not to harm his little friends. But the cruel eagle drops the clover carrying the speck in a great patch of clovers hundreds of miles wide.

Poor Horton searches the field, examining every clover and calling out to his friend, the mayor, until he has picked three million flowers. Exhausted but joyous, Horton finally finds the dust speck. The other animals have now had quite enough. They decide to rope and cage him and boil the speck in oil. Horton pleads with the people of Whoville to speak up, to make themselves heard. Even though all of the townspeople scream as loudly as they can, the other animals still cannot hear the Who.

They imprison Horton, beat him, and tie him up with ropes. Despite this treatment, Horton continues to insist that his friends are alive and living on the speck. He is adamant about his convictions and willing to die for them. Finally, the mayor of Whoville, knowing that this is the town's darkest hour, finds just one small child, who climbs to the top of a tower and yells as hard as he can.

Suddenly, the other animals in the jungle hear. That one small voice makes the difference, and now they all finally know it is true. There really is a Whoville. They all vow to protect the town from that day forth. Horton is set free and becomes a hero.

This is a lovely fairy tale about both the divinely abnormal and the power of the individual. Because Horton was gifted with very large ears, he was able to hear things that others could not. Because of his "equipment," he had access to another level of sound beyond the range of the others. It is the same for us. We need only to fine-tune our human machinery to be able to pierce the façade that we think separates us from the vast and unequaled beauty of other dimensional realms.

For reasons still not clear to me, my consciousness had entered the nebulous portal into these regions, and I was able to perceive things not perceptible through the ordinary five senses. Like Horton, when I discussed my unusual insights with my peers, I was ostracized and ridiculed. Unlike Horton, I did not initially have unwavering faith in my perceptions. The story of Horton is a great, yet simplistic example of the divinely abnormal.

Whether the story is about a person living in contemporary time, such as Barry, a historical figure such as Joan of Arc, or a fairy tale character such as Horton, each portrays the divinely abnormal and the burdens that may accompany such a gift.

What if mystical consciousness and direct communication with individuals living in other dimensional realms became accepted and "normal?" Just imagine the conversation. "Oh, did you hear about Lois? She was talking to her Mentor the other day and got some really great advice!"

Humanity just has to take one colossal leap of faith, and that imaginary chat will soon become a reality!

Finding Yourself
Means Finding Everyone Else

> *"See the world as yourself. Have faith in the way things are. Love the world as yourself; Then you can care for all things."*
>
> —Lao-tzu

nd so the curious story of my first encounter with Universal Mind concludes here. It is both a cherished completion and the inauguration of a new and pivotal life genesis. As I cast an anchor carefully sculpted from ironclad faith and heave it into the oceanic providence of God, it plunges through the surface and is submerged into the deepest regions of divinity. It remains there, tethered only by my devout passion and tenacious determination to remain intimate with my Source.

It now seems to be an opportune time to gather together the knowledge I have gained about the inter-relationship between humanity and the Universe, between the microcosm and the Macrocosm, and translate those realizations into action. Inevitably, in the course of all personal growth, concerns about our own individual evolution must ultimately yield to the recognition of the greater importance of the evolution of the Whole. At this time, we need to turn our attention away from self-centeredness and begin to seek a greater Center.

I have finally begun to comprehend the troublesome obstacles and barriers that hinder most of us from being able to access mystical realms, from seeing Reality. Knowing and expressing our soul's nature should be so natural. Why is it not?

The answer lies in the regrettable fact that we have digressed into a society that is so utterly disconnected from a sense of community, from nature, from ourselves, and our Source. We have become obsessively engrossed with our emotional wounds, frenzied attempts to bolster sagging egos, personal daily melodramas, the unlimited desire for material things, and the fruitless search in all the wrong places for happiness, meaning, and purpose. Turning our attention away from these unproductive preoccupations to more pragmatic aspirations can transmute a life of mediocrity into magic.

The experiences that I have had, although stupefying, have occurred since the dawn of humankind and are emerging with greater frequency now than ever before. Consciousness is what we truly are and is what remains when we are finished with this particular lifetime. Experiencing our true selves should not be considered an impossible dream.

What stands in the way? What exactly do we need to do to nourish, nurture, and support mystical consciousness or contact with the soul? The quest to know God is not to be taken lightly. The ability to contact the place inside yourself that is a fragment of the Whole can be developed, but it will require numerous and perhaps radical changes in your life, a tremendous amount of discipline, and exceedingly sincere intention.

❧❧ Seven Suggestions for the Soul: Seeking Your Source

Through the years, I have found a number of practical exercises that can be enormously helpful in crossing the threshold that leads to higher states of consciousness. The degree to which you are dedicated to these principles and open-heartedly strive to live a spiritual life is the degree to which you will reap the restorative benefits. I have prepared an outline, a relief map to follow. It addresses the most basic and fundamental requirements and is intended to be merely a starting point. I hope that it is helpful.

I. Live Every Day with Awareness

Exercise One. Learn to awaken the slumbering parts of yourself. Remember that your soul is the true and unquestionable proprietor of your body. Throughout the day, from the time you wake up in the morning to the moment you fall asleep, train yourself to be fully alert mentally, intuitively, and spiritually. Visualize yourself and everyone around you as we really are, immortal beings of light, all born from the same light Source. For example, when driving in traffic, release the stressful us-versus-them mentality and tell yourself, "Relax, there is only US."

Exercise Two. Pay attention to and follow the deeper, inherent instinctive perceptions that spring spontaneously from either soul awareness or guidance from your Mentor. Remember that everything already exists in the universe in some unfathomable realm. We only have to be inspired and imagine it. For example, atomic energy has always existed, but in the absence of conscious realization, we cannot avail ourselves of its use. Listen to the inner voice that provocatively fans the flames of revelation.

Exercise Three. Try the following simple exercise to develop conscious observing. Arrange a quiet time and place. Take several deep breaths and fully relax. Pick out an object in nature or in your home that is common to you but usually goes unnoticed. It can be a piece of fruit, a leaf, a vase, an insect, or a flower (something in nature is preferable). Get very close to it and concentrate your undivided attention upon this object with the fervid intention of looking at it as if it were the very first time.

Toss out of your mind any preconceived notions and delve passionately and without reservation into its substance. Look through the eyes of your soul. Use your inner vision. Permit no distractions to divert your focus. Most likely, you will begin to expose the complex and intricate details and subtle qualities that make this item unique. Try to appreciate the miraculous and distinctive human or divine intelligence behind its creation. If it is manufactured, think about the person that crafted it and the many people that participated in its production. If it is a tree, contemplate the way the tree breathes, inhaling carbon dioxide and exhaling oxygen, and the symbiotic relationship between you and this entity from the plant world. Envision its origin, a tiny seed, and the profound ingenuity behind the construction of all the elaborate and ornate flora.

Attempt to use all of your senses when viewing this object. Not only see it, but if possible, smell, touch, and taste it. Ponder any effect it might have on you as you examine it. Express gratitude for its existence. Remind yourself that it is composed of the same atomic substance as yourself and, therefore, is a part of you.

If you use the same introspective method to contemplate yourself, you may begin to infiltrate into the depths of your own miraculous interior core. Therein lies the same complex and intricate design and details that you appreciated in the object. You might see both your beauty and your flaws. Do not be afraid to take stock of both assets and liabilities. Search your heart. Search your soul.

In practicing deep contemplation and applying it to your daily life, you are training yourself to "see." It will shift your vision to such a degree that even the most ordinary things and yourself will be revealed as having sacred and celestial qualities.

Exercise Four. Remain fully aware that absolutely EVERYTHING that exists is here to benefit humanity. This is the ultimate endowment and blessing bestowed to us from an unconditionally benevolent Source. It might exist to aid in our survival or simply to bring beauty into our lives. There is nothing that you can see or touch that was not created to assist and support us. Hold that thought in your mind with appreciation always. Turn off your "automatic-pilot" system and remember to walk with Universal Mind in great reverence, realization, and recognition.

Exercise Five. See the chi or "dancing air" all around you. With patience and concentration, you can observe this miracle of nature. On a sunny day with a clear sky (it is much more difficult when cloudy), face directly away from the sun and focus your eyes a few feet away from yourself. Relax and stay focused on the brightness of the sky and these luminescent specks should shortly come into view.

II. Practice Harmlessness

Exercise One. Make a commitment, as a resolute ideal, not to harm another living thing, including yourself. Do not cause any injury, whether in words or deeds. Even negative thoughts are harmful because they are physical energy. Maintain a state of mind that vigilantly monitors and appraises your thoughts and emotions so that it incorporates, as much as possible, a loving and compassionate attitude.

Exercise Two. Make a special effort not to damage anything in nature and protect it as you would your own child. We are the caretakers of the Earth and are responsible for its well-being and health. In return, it will cooperatively provide a cornucopia of abundance for us all.

Exercise Three. Practice forgiveness. Realize that other people's hurtful behavior is not meant to be personal. You may just happen to be in the line of fire of someone's momentary or chronic imbalance. Holding on to resentments and hostility is mostly toxic to the person generating them.

Exercise Four. Always tell the truth, no matter what the situation. Lies are always harmful, even to your health. Lie detectors are able to ferret out deceit because lies cause a rift between our soul, which cannot lie, and our personality, which can. Our biochemistry and overall physiology is altered because lying goes against our true nature. Everything that we do that goes against our spirit and the natural forces is detrimental to us.

Exercise Five. Avoid all mind pollution. Refuse to participate in society's infatuation with violence as entertainment. Refrain from all films and television that idealize and romanticize hurting other people. This can profoundly affect your biochemistry by causing a multitude of stresses that actually change the physical structure and chemistry of your brain. When you watch a violent movie and are stressed by it, harmful hormones are secreted, particularly corticotrophin, the master stress hormone. Essential cells are damaged, and pathways between brain regions necessary for memory can be broken. Continuing to submit yourself to a bombardment of visual violence is just not conducive to higher states of consciousness and is also potentially quite harmful to your physiology.

Prolonged and frequent exposure to violence causes children to become desensitized and view aberrant acts as "normal." The average American child watches eight thousand murders and one hundred thousand acts of violence by the time he or she leaves elementary school. Repeatedly viewing images of savage and murderous people encourages children to eventually reflect that image. The popular science fiction movie "Cocoon," produced by Ron Howard, is about intelligent, peaceful, angelic, and telepathic light beings. That image is certainly closer to the truth about who we are. The more definite and precise we are to ourselves and to our children about the truth of our real nature, the easier it is to actually manifest and personify.

III. Listen to the Language of Universal Mind

Those who have had a feeling or the realization of the presence of Universal Mind are no longer alone in the world. They no longer need to work out problems bereft of guidance. The knowledge that the Divine is present in everything and is our constant escort and counsel can eliminate the painful feeling of loneliness. With awareness and sensitivity, look for the signposts, syncronicity, and symbols that are the beacons of light you are to follow. Walk alongside the trail of footprints and fingerprints that are the residue of divine grace. They will speak to you in the form of dreams, events, and nature. Listen carefully and consistently.

Begin to shift your awareness so that you are able to view life as a metaphor, as continual symbolic messages that teach lessons through allegorical events. Remember that Universal Mind speaks to us directly, but in cryptic, metaphorical language. Learn to interpret objects and experiences as having their own special and unique meaning just for you. This task of unveiling the hidden truths requires a state of mind that is open, receptive, and nonjudgmental.

Yield and surrender to the natural flow of life rather than trying to control it. Incorporate the affirmation "Thy will, not my will," into daily life.

IV. Simplify

Practice voluntary simplicity. Try to keep in mind that we do not really "own" anything, not the property that we purchased, or even our body. Everything is just loaned to us during each brief residency in the physical world. Certainly, you cannot take anything with you when your time here is finished. Reevaluate your priorities to generate a high quality of inner life, not an excessive quantity of possessions. Discover the freedom in living a simple life. Make your mental, physical, and spiritual health of paramount importance.

It is virtually impossible to have happiness, joy, and peace of mind without a genuine and firmly established sense of self-worth. Direct your efforts and energy to the accumulation of interior wealth by identifying yourself as a child of God rather than by external accessories or your profession. Train yourself to slow down. It is not possible to maintain awareness while rushing through life.

V. Mind The Body, Mend The Mind

Attention to this practice is more essential than most people realize. Treat your body as a sacred sanctuary because that is what it is. Your physical form is the clothing and vehicle for your soul's expression.

It is important to be physically in sync with nature, but unfortunately, Western society has departed from the diet that we were clearly meant to have. We are provided with everything that we need—nutrition-rich vegetables, grains, and roots from the earth; fruit from the trees; fish from the sea; and fresh water to drink. Nonetheless, we have become disconnected even from our food source upon which we depend for survival. Foods sprayed with toxic pesticides, harvested and then saturated with yet more potentially lethal chemicals, and finally bombarded with radiation are probably not exactly what God had in mind at the time of creation. These practices, which are now standard operating procedure, destroy the life force within the food and stress our bodies. Unchecked, they will eventually obliterate us with a proliferation of existing and new diseases.

This is yet another example of how we are drifting away from what is normal and natural. The further we stray from the life that nature intended, the further we are from becoming deeply allied with our Source. Refuse to dishonor your own body by striving to maintain a healthful dietary regime free of all chemicals.

Make sure to get plenty of exercise, rest, and sunshine.

VI. Meditation, Solitude, and Prayer

Meditation

Meditation is, by far, the most beneficial spiritual practice. Daily meditation is the best method of paving the way for deepening self knowledge, making direct contact with your own spirit, and moving into closer rapport with our Mentors and Universal Mind. Developing a penchant toward routine meditation expedites raising the lower, more primitive energies (such as survival instincts) into elevated, strengthening forces and aids in the refinement of the transmutation process. It synergizes the alignment of the soul and the personality so that they are coordinated and may work together more harmoniously.

Meditation accelerates the achievement of a consistently balanced inner equilibrium and increases access to higher consciousness. It is the most effective approach to seeking your Source. Daily practice promotes sensations of calm, unity, transcendence, and spiritual sensitivity, which are then translated into improved physical health.

Set aside fifteen minutes once a day if you are just beginning, or thirty minutes if you have experience with meditation. Morning is best. Wake up earlier if necessary. Choose a quiet place, preferably the same location each time so that your own personal electromagnetic energy builds and accumulates in that area and facilitates the following meditation.

In complete silence, choose a comfortable and serene seated position. If necessary, use back support and fold your hands loosely in your lap. With your eyes closed, take several deep breaths. Concentrate on the fact that you are physically part of the divine consciousness and are simply seeking to merge with your higher self and your Source, which is one and the same thing. Withdraw into the true nature of the Self.

Exercise One. After you have completely relaxed, visualize a closed, white, iridescent flower with hundreds of petals in the center of your chest over your heart. Imagine it slowly expanding and opening as a whirling mixture of electric blue and gold light swirls around and through it. Try to hold the image for several minutes.

Exercise Two. Concentrate on the virtue that you yearn for the most. Now, focus your attention on the attainment of that virtue. Each month, for one year, continue to add additional qualities until you have clearly erected a concept of your ideal self. Instead of looking externally for someone who embodies the standard of excellence that you admire, create those assets that are important to you within yourself.

Exercise Three. Concentrate on your breathing for fifteen minutes. Direct your thinking to watching the inhalations and exhalations calmly and objectively.

Exercise Four. Do nothing. Think nothing. Just be.

Reaping the benefits of meditation requires patience and perseverance. Prolonged and consistent effort is the key to progress. There are no shortcuts. The ultimate goal of meditation is the eventual ability to control the mind so that it is not an emotionally fueled "runaway train." Then it is possible to remain in a meditative state of unity and awareness throughout the day and weave this sense of affinity into the fabric of daily life.

Solitude

Paradoxically, when we are in solitude, we are least alone. In solitude, there is a better likelihood of collaborating and converging with yourself and your Source. What takes place within us when we are by ourselves is just as important as what takes place during interpersonal relationships and should be equally valued and sought after. When distractions are eliminated, it can be a time when distinguishing latent and creative qualities can spring forth and be brought into expression. It is a time that is pregnant with possibility.

In the silence of solitude, it is easier to firmly establish and strengthen the all-important "vertical relationships" with your Mentors and Universal Mind. These timeless relationships, which symbolically ascend upward, are immutable and unwavering. All other relationships in the physical world, or "horizontal relationships," which are figuratively linear and on a level plane are also vitally important, but, typically, not as steady and unconditional. Horizontal relationships thrive by nurturing them with time, devotion, and love. Vertical relationships also thrive with the same effort, but the difference is that they are best fostered in solitude.

Make time for both kinds of relationships, the temporal and the celestial, and acknowledge them equally. Be alone to learn that you are not alone.

Prayer

Prayer is a deeply intimate act. It is a linking up of minds—your own unique and individual mind with the Universal Mind. It is union with your Source. Although group prayer may involve many people, it may be even more powerful than solitary prayer because the fellowship of the group enhances the recognition of the universality of everyone and everything.

Let all of life be a prayer. Miracles can happen. Pray for them. Have faith that Universal Mind registers and responds to your thoughts. Speak to your Source with the expectation of having a dialogue. Be receptive. Whenever afraid, pray for assistance in transmuting fear into faith. Pray with an ear of expectancy. Yearn to know your Source with an unquenchable desire.

There is no more potent and fertile time for spiritual emergence than in the stillness and quiet of meditation, solitude, and prayer.

VII. Serve Humanity

Practice goodwill. You might ask yourself the questions, "Who can I help?" and "What should be done?" Service to others need not consist of momentous acts that change the world. The simplest and most spontaneous things can make a tangible difference. Opening the door for someone, smiling at a stranger, and letting someone ahead of you in line are subtle and random acts of kindness that have the potential to transform you and the world around you. Notice how you feel when you help someone or something in need. Serving humanity is the crowning ingredient in the recipe for the meaning and purpose of life.

Service to others is an activity that is a reflexive exhibition of the soul. It is our true nature expressed in behavior. The natural impulses of the soul are as strong or stronger than the inherent reproductive instincts of the body. Repressing either one can result in unhealthy and adverse repercussions.

Turn your attention toward making others happy rather than yourself. Focus on giving love rather than receiving it. Giving is far more rewarding. Serve by spreading joy. That act alone may render a great and profound assistance to others.

Imagine yourself at age one hundred, sitting in a rocking chair pondering your life and just about to leave the physical world. What would you like to say about the contribution you have made to humanity in your lifetime? Your first thought is the most important one. Follow through on it and fulfill your dreams. Whatever you can envision, you can accomplish.

Every night, review the events of your day. How would you regard the day's accomplishments? Ask yourself, "If everyone were just like me, what kind of world would it be?" Visualize a utopian world. Then, live as if you were an integral part of it.

Perhaps you have already incorporated many of these suggestions successfully into your life but still have not experienced direct communion with Universal Mind. Please be patient. It is important not to focus on those specific results, but rather on changing your life so that your spiritual-mindedness is translated into consistent behavior that reflects your true nature and essence. Most important are the quality of the life you are leading and the continuous evolution of your soul.

All circumstances in life present a golden opportunity to act divinely. These seven suggestions are meant to provide just some of the practical passageways to discovering the nexus between yourself and the mysterious link that unites us all. Finding yourself will mean that you will find everyone else. When you accomplish this, you will also come face to face with your Source.

Epilogue

> *"There are no unnatural or supernatural phenomena, only very large gaps in our knowledge of what is natural.... We should strive to fill those gaps of ignorance."*
> —*Edgar Mitchell, Apollo 14 Astronaut*

This book begins by asking a question. Were the impromptu events that I experienced a result of madness or mysticism? Was the entry into the multifaceted, mosaic passageway of the divine world akin to striking a reverberating chord in the chorus of the Maestro's symphony? Did I see an infinite number of orchestrated, singular dots all meticulously arranged like an impressionistic painting to form one cohesive totality, the living embodiment of an incalculable intelligence? Or was the entirety of my experiences just the random echo of a collage of unbridled yearnings seeping from a deteriorated and fractured psyche?

I asked myself those questions hundreds of times during the years following my first walk with Universal Mind. The answer that eventually materialized lives deep within my heart. The experience that I had can only be conveyed in terms of beauty, grace, and intelligence. It is like seeing the artistry of the greatest master painter, feeling the gentle stroking of the wind, hearing the tender whisper of the most sublime music.

As a result of weathering the trials and tribulations during this personal pilgrimage of the spirit, these writings emerged. It is my hope that through them a foundation has been laid to assist you in finding your own answer. Is it fact or fiction that there is an inconceivable, unfathomable intelligence that permeates the universe and by whose directive we must live?

Throughout all of my uncertainty, angst, and skepticism and all of the suffering and inner feuds, in the deepest reaches of my soul I always knew that part of the reason we are here, part of our purpose, is to unravel life's great mysteries. The teeming, transcendent wonders of life are not cloaked to an open and questioning mind.

With resolute determination, I ventured on a profound trek over stony terrain that both rose to the greatest heights and plunged to the lowest depths. The transformation that occurred during this mercurial odyssey resulted in the gentle brushing of ornate gilding over unrefined wood. My discoveries made life all the more exquisite and precious and ablaze with rhapsodic mystique. But in the bigger picture, in the course of infinite and indestructible spiritual evolution, these incidents are just a flicker on the screen of life.

The most important realization and understanding came when I recognized that what is truly essential and fundamental to life is invisible to the physical eye, but not to spiritual sight. That almost seems like a cruel paradox, the fact that we are meant to have to search, labor, and struggle just to perceive and know something that is not only right in front of us, but wholly within us. But who are we to question nature and the way things were originally designed? Nature always directs us to our origin. Unfortunately, we often disregard the road signs.

Over the years, I have repeatedly asked myself, "What does it mean to live a spiritual life?" The answer is this: A spiritual life is a sane life. Spirituality is sanity.

I am certainly not speaking in clinical terms, but rather defining sanity in terms of the degree of separation from what is normal and natural. Just as criminals irrationally believe that they can break society's laws and get away with it, it is lunacy to think that we can violate and infringe upon every law of nature and not suffer the consequences.

The further we are from living in unison and cooperation with Nature, the more problems we create for ourselves. We have spawned innumerable and senseless predicaments and opened a virtual Pandora's Box of potential destruction, and all because of our misguided desires and perceptions. What is sorely needed is not just a change in lifestyle, but first and foremost, a change in attitude.

Perhaps one last story will illustrate the importance of this point.

It was several days before the Christmas holiday and, as usual, everyone was frenetically bustling about the city finishing work, maneuvering through the crowds to buy gifts, and in perpetual motion completing endless chores. It seemed as if the whole world was accelerated and in a fast-forward mode.

I was on an errand at an office building that wraps around a large waterway originating at the bay. Every winter, herds of manatees congregate in this winding, grass-green channel in an attempt to flee the chilly open waters to stay warm. On this particular day, seven manatees were in the canal. They were of all different sizes, and the group was obviously made up of several families. These gentle-hearted, sweet-tempered animals must be among the most hilarious-looking creatures ever dreamed up by nature. Full-grown, they resemble eight-foot-long, plump Cuban cigars with flippers. But appearance aside, their eyes reflect something that is not seen in other animals—a completely defenseless innocence, an unguarded, yet wise vulnerability.

I stood on a small bridge, leaning against the railing overlooking the water and watching these tender, graceful creatures as they nuzzled each other and lovingly nursed their young. Completely mesmerized by the manatees, I was in the process of making eye contact and a mental connection with one of them when a woman hurriedly burst out of an office and rushed past me. Out of the corner of my eye, I could see that she had abruptly stopped sprinting, pivoted, retraced her steps, and was approaching me. Her arms were laden with papers, files, and a heavy briefcase, all piled up to her chin. Breathless and perspiring profusely, she appeared quite harried and overwrought.

"What are you doing? What are you looking at?" she queried in a most insistent manner.

"Just watching the manatees," I replied.

She stared at me almost in disbelief. "I have heard about them. Are they fish or reptiles?"

"Neither," I answered. "Mammals. Do you work here?"

She was becoming somewhat more amicable. "Yes, I've worked as a real estate broker in this building for nine years, but I have never had the time to come out here, so I have never seen them."

She told me her name was Maria. I saw my old self mirrored in her face as she uttered the words "no time." For some reason which I will never know, she put down her papers on the sidewalk and we stood on that bridge for almost an hour and talked about life, God, and the many marvels of nature.

Her expression gradually changed from flustered and taut to collected and calm. After an exchange of business cards, with a warm smile, she was on her way.

As I stood on that bridge enjoying my manatees, I watched her walk away, now strolling.

Maria is the personification of urban insanity. She was a lovely woman, insightful, energetic, and full of life. But in nine years, she had been too busy "working" to even notice the magnificent endangered species right in her back yard.

Where are we putting our attention and why have we become so alienated from what is natural and inborn? They are difficult questions to answer, but possibly this book has helped you in some small way to find and follow the upward spiraling road that will usher you to solutions and to your Source.

The early experiences that I had were by far the most intense to date. They were the initial wake-up call and the premiere of the apex of a life that is lived with great hope for both myself and for all of humanity. The evolutionary process promises to continue yielding a growing revelation that we all are, indeed, physically part of one collective form. You and I are not just related, but commingle within the same primordial pool of atoms. Perhaps soon, the horror of what we do to each other will cease, and the nobility of the human spirit will permanently awaken and tilt toward creating a world that is finally at peace.

We are all perpetual travelers timelessly navigating the twists and turns of the winding and rocky paths of life. Like wandering nomads, we may journey down this sacred and endless road unable to see our destination, so mysterious and unknown. But no matter how many crossroads we encounter, regardless of stormy weather and shattered dreams, inevitably, all paths are entryways that must eventually lead to the Center, back to the Source, and back to the Known.

I wish you joy and serenity on this miraculous journey, and remember…

Always keep the light, even in the darkness.

Resources

American Psychiatric Association. 1994. *Diagnostic and Statistical Manual of Mental Disorders: DSM-IV, 4th ed.* Washington, D.C.: American Psychiatric Association.

Bailey, Alice A. 1987. *Serving Humanity*. New York: Lucis Publishing Company.

Geisel, Theodore Seuss (pseud. Dr. Seuss). 1954. *Horton Hears a Who*. New York: Random House.

James, William. 1961. *The Varieties of Religious Experience*. New York: Macmillan.

Jung, Carl G. 1953. "Synchronicity: An Acausal Connecting People." In *The Collected Works of C. G. Jung*. Eds., Herbert Read, Michael Fordham, and Gerhard Adler. New York: Pantheon Books.

Seigel, Bernie S. 1986. *Love, Medicine, and Miracles*. New York: Harper and Row.

Weiss, Brian L. 1996. *Many Lives, Many Masters*. New York: Warner Books.